Pet, Animal Welfare and Wildlife Funding:

300+ Grants, Scholarships and More

in the U.S. and Canada

Authored By:
PAMELA BURKE

ISBN-13: 978-1511472371

ISBN-10:1511472375

CONTENTS

ACKNOWLEDGEMENTS

Authored By:
PAMELA BURKE, LLC
GRANTS CONSULTANT ~ FUND DEVELOPMENT + GRANT
RESEARCH/WRITING
Over 35 years experience
Improving the quality of life for communities by building organizational capacity
Phone (989) 330-1678; Email info@grant-write.com;
website www.grant-write.com

Research editing by Clara Bauman - dadsit90@gmail.com
Graphic Design by Audrea DeLong - asd.design35@gmail.com
Running Dogs Cover Photo by Frank Youngman -
spiritofsuperior@gmail.com

Printed by CreateSpace, an Amazon.com Company;
Available from Amazon.com, CreateSpace.com, and,
through www.grant-write.com.

INTRODUCTION:

All across North America groups are working to save animals, provide care and recognize their value in our lives. We depend on animals and they depend on us. Animals bring us unconditional love, joy and comfort. Who doesn't love to watch a newborn goat kid frolicking? Or chuckle at a naughty puppy? Or watch dogs running free? Animals also provide us with wool, eggs, milk and hours of recreation such as horseback riding. Pets become family members. They need us to keep them safe and healthy. Pet, animal and wildlife groups have an abundance of passion – but finding funding for projects is often an issue. Community groups, nonprofit organizations, students and local governments can use this book to find funding sources that may help with spay/neuter programs, health care, shelters, companion programs, rescues, education, preserves and more.

USING THE FUNDING DIRECTORY & WRITING A GRANT

The purpose of this directory is to **save you hundreds of hours** searching for funders who have shown an interest in your cause. Funders can be foundations, trusts, funds within community foundations, corporate giving programs, associations, nonprofit organizations and governmental agencies. Funding may be available in the form of a loan, a grant, a donation, a contract for services, a cooperative agreement, or a scholarship.

Consider the odds. If a funder publishes that there will only be four awards made during the year (as opposed to 40), unless your project is exactly what the funder wishes to support, the odds of getting awarded diminishes. Because there are many more nonprofits seeking funding than there are funders, grant funding should be only one of your sources of revenue. Most funders like to invest in established organizations; fewer funders make awards to new nonprofits or wish to pay for operating day to day costs.

Increase your odds. Study your funder before applying. Follow the funder's directions. Make sure the contact person's information is clearly included. Make sure your math is correct. Do your homework to make sure the funder's passion is your passion – How much do they typically award? How many awards were made last year? And where?

If you have the opportunity to speak or correspond with the funder, please do so. Ask the funder to describe the best project ever funded – the one that makes them most proud. Run your idea past them before you put in a great deal of effort. Confirm the deadline and how the funder wants it to be submitted (Send a letter of inquiry first briefly describing the project and then wait for an invitation? Send by email? Online form? Typed? Certain font? Single spaced or doubled? Limit on the number of pages allowed? By U.S. mail or another mail delivery service (and are there different addresses such as a P.O. Box or a street address.) Delivered by a certain date and time? Signature in ink or will an electronic signature work? Multiple copies? Multiple copies of proposal but just one set of attachments?) Also ask, when is the start date and when is the end date. All funders have different grant periods which often do not match your organization's fiscal year.

First things first...are you eligible? Each funder will state who is eligible for their grants. Most grants are awarded to nonprofit organizations or local governments for charitable or educational purposes. Sometimes a local government or nonprofit is the applicant on behalf of a group; the nonprofit may write a for-profit business or provider (farm, animal rescue, etc.) or group of providers into the grant project as contractual providers. Scholarships are usually awarded to individuals. Loans and contracts may be available to individuals, for-profit businesses/providers and nonprofit organizations.

Is your organization ready to apply for a grant? Grant readiness is key. Funders may ask for certain documents to be included with your proposal so that they can determine your organization's readiness and management competence. Do you or your fiduciary have paper and/or digitized copies of your organization's legal, governance and financial documents at the ready? These may include the organizational EIN#, 501c3 letter, Financial Statement/Audit, Annual Budget, and Board Roster? Some funders may also ask to see some of these: By-Laws, Articles of Incorporation, DUNS #, Proof of Liability Insurance, Fund Development/ Donor recognition plan, Staff bios/Resumes', Organizational Chart, Mission/values statement, and/or, an Annual Report. I suggest scanning these docs and keeping them in a folder in the computer for easy retrieval. You will also look use these docs for certain information required on online application forms, for filling out paper grant forms, or, as Attachments.   Does your organization have the skills and resources to manage a grant? Does your organization have the ability to track restricted funds in your bookkeeping system?

When writing a grant, keep in mind that you are competing against many other applicants. Don't assume that the grant reviewer understands your community or your system. Make sure there are no misspelled words. Make sure that all acronyms are defined. And that information follows logically. It is important to use words that "paint a picture" for the reader when describing the community to be served, the setting and the problem to be solved. You will then explain your proposed solution to the problem and what resources and expertise your organization will use to address it.

Research is the first step in finding funding. Locating funders that may be interested in your cause, your activity and location can be extremely time consuming. After circling the best prospective funders, do even more research by reading the funder's website – especially their "About Us" section, Giving Guidelines, and past awardees. Their annual reports will also provide information about the approaches they most often support.

Awards are made to satisfy the donor's desire. Keep in mind that you are not only seeking a grant to enhance your program to better serve your community, but to **meet the funder's intended purpose.** Note those funders that provide funding *where* you wish to operate your program, that are interested in *what* you wish to accomplish and *when.*

Look for those whose application process meets your timeline.
One to six months can pass between the day you submit your
application and the date of the funder's response. And your
official start date can be even later. So think ahead and try to seek
funding for your next fiscal year.

Some funders reserve most or all of their awards to certain
STATES or *PROVINCES*. If funders in this directory restrict their
awards geographically these are shown in CAPS.

Also note that some funders may only accept grants during
certain windows of time, may have deadlines or giving cycles.
Funders may change their deadlines and application processes so
check their website and follow the instructions as published.
Once you find some funders in the directory with whom you have
a connection you can begin building a quarterly calendar. If
possible begin working on the grant in the quarter before the
expected due date.

Funders make grants and scholarship awards to promote the
cause near and dear to them. Look for funders with whom you
sense a connection. As you review the entries in this directory,
look for those that best match your ideals, proposed activity, your
approach, and, geographic area of interest.

Grants tend to follow the same general order. You may wish to begin with a powerful attention getting statement. Example: "The food safety of meat, milk, cheese and eggs is threatened by the shortage of veterinarians treating farm animals in the state. Some estimates say that only one out of forty practicing vets currently treat farm animals." And include the source, according to Brown & Young, 2014.....

Grant proposals generally contain the following:

The issue, problem, or need,

Who is impacted, how many/where, and who will benefit,

Who you are (about your organization, mission/values, governance, service area/community, experience),

What (proposed solution, goal/objectives, desired outcomes),

How (activities, who will do what to whom and how often, the process),

When (project start & end date, timeline),

How much (costs, resources, the $ request), how you will measure success (process, outputs, outcomes),

Impact/Sustainability,

Staffing/Chances of Succeeding (Credentials? Memberships? Staff expertise and training? Who will supervise? Systems in place? Partnerships?) .

Some examples of problems that your proposal may seek to address:

ANIMAL PROBLEMS	
Over-population	Sick care days versus total care days
Shortage of spay/neutering clinics	Social benefit/human comfort
# of euthanized healthy animals	Lack of day care services
Lack of foster homes	Abandoned pets
Feral Cats	Danger to wildlife
Wild dogs, dog packs	Abused animals
Safety to children/adults	Disaster related issues
Pets/livestock attacked	Low income with limited vet care, food, etc.
Communicable diseases/conditions	Transition to sustainable practices
Feral animals causing property damage	Lack of awareness/knowledge
Lack of shelter space	Waste
Shelter overcrowding	Overhead costs
# of homeless animals	Reduced Habitat
Unplanned litters	Lack of collaboration
Lack of access, Limited days/hours	Poor economy/lack of jobs
Costs to community	Aggressive behavior
Standards not met	Need for food, vaccines, cleaning supplies.

Prepare a project budget. Not all funders will support the same expenses. Some will contribute only toward education or training while another may only fund supplies or equipment costs. Be sure to note each funder's **allowable costs**. And check whether the funder wants to see local match (other funds committed or pending for this project.) Project budgets may include these categories:

CATEGORY	DETAIL/QUANTITY	GRANT SHARE	OTHER FUNDING	TOTAL
Personnel	6 hours/week x $10 x 10 weeks	$300	$300	$600
Fringe	15%	$45	$45	$90
Travel	60 miles x 10 weeks x .50	$100	$200	$300
Supplies	6 crates x $50/each	$100	$200	$300
Equipment	1 Scale	$300	$0	$300
Contractual				
Construction				
Other				
Total Expenses		**$845**	**$745**	**$1,590**
% Expenses		**53% Grant**	**47% Match**	**100%**

Some grants will also require a budget justification or narrative explanation as to why each expenses is necessary and reasonable. And a list of other funders and resources being used to carry out the project.

If you are awarded, the funder will expect that the award funding be used to satisfy the funder's purpose and as described in the proposal or application submitted unless the funder is willing to allow slight changes to the plan. Be sure to send a thank you letter to the funder within two weeks of the award. You may wish to ask for their logo and exact wording to be used when publicizing the award on your website or in your newsletter.

You should also be prepared to issue a press release to the media, prepare and send a mid-year and a final report discussing the process, inputs, outputs and outcomes. The reports should discuss whether the proposed tasks were completed according to the original proposal, whether the numbers of those who were expected to be impacted were served and whether the anticipated outcomes were achieved. You may also wish to provide the funder with project photos that can be used in their newsletter, webpage and annual report.

If not funded, don't give up. Please know that even excellent proposals may be turned down! Seeking grants is part art, part science and part luck of the draw! A denial can be an opportunity to strengthen the proposal. You may get turned down multiple times before winning an award from a funder. It is worth noting that you or your grant writer cannot control many of the elements that impact giving. Some decision makers may have connections to some of the applicants – including those that build relationships before applying and past awardees who have performed well on past grants by this funder. Some of the other applicants may have had greater need and evidence of that need.

THE DIRECTORY

THE HOWARD J. & DOROTHY ADLETA FOUNDATION

The Foundation is independent and provides grant support for a number of causes in Dallas and Fort Worth TEXAS including animal welfare. Nonprofit organizations should submit a proposal including a copy of IRS Determination Letter, statement of problem project will address, detailed description of project and amount of funding requested and brief history of organization and description of its mission. Deadline is August 1. Mail proposal to: The Howard J and Dorothy Adleta Foundation, c/o Frost National Bank, Attn: Bonnie Swindall, 8201 Preston Road Suite 180, Dallas, TX 75225-6206.

AHIMSA FOUNDATION

The Foundation supports organization involved in the care and protection of animals and related activities. Past charitable organization awardees include rescues, sanctuaries, advocacy organizations across the U.S. Write c/o John K Graham, Esq. 60 State Street, Suite 700, Boston, MA 02109.

ALEXANDER FOUNDATION

Provides grants up to $5,000 for general and operating support for animal welfare and sanctuaries nationwide. No deadlines. Send a letter of inquiry by mail at any time to Edythe M. Alexander, Director, 1255 Cherry Tree Lane, Annapolis, MD 21403.

ALLEN FOUNDATION
Supports charitable purposes including funding prevention of cruelty to animals in the State of WISCONSIN. Deadlines February 1, June 1 and October 1. The Foundation is administered by the J.P. Morgan is part of JPMorgan Chase & Co. Applications must be submitted online.
See:
www.jpmorgan.com/pages/jpmorgan/private_banking/fo undations/online_grant_application/search

ALTERNATIVES RESEARCH AND DEVELOPMENT FOUNDATION (ARDF)
The foundation funds and promotes alternatives to the use of laboratory animals in research, testing and education. They wish to fund and promote the development, validation and adoption of non-animal methods in biomedical research, product testing and education. Individual projects, preference to U.S. universities and research institutions, up to $40,000. April deadline.
See: www.ardf-online.org/

AMERICAN ASSOCIATION OF BOVINE PRACTITIONERS (AABP)
The goal of the AABP is to support veterinary students and students just entering veterinary medicine in completing a bovine externship. There are a number of other sponsored awards and scholarships to promote beef and dairy health studies. Deadlines in the fall and spring.
See: http://www.aabp.org/students/asep.asp

AMERICAN ASSOCIATION OF EQUINE PRACTITIONERS (AAEP)

Supports charitable purposes including funding projects that positively impact the health and welfare of horses – on a national or international level. Four goals for funding are research, education, leadership and actual health of horses. The group also makes disaster relief awards and gives scholarships to equine vet and research grad students. Download instructions & applications. Submit early spring. See: www.aaep.org

AMERICAN HUMANE ASSOCIATION

The following grant opportunities are offered through American Humane Association to animal welfare agencies - when funding allows. The Meacham Foundation Memorial Grant funds capital campaigns, building improvements, and equipment purchases that directly affect the welfare of animals in shelters with grants up to $4,000. Applicants must be a 501 (c)(3) nonprofit agency. The Second Chance Fund gives animal victims of abuse or neglect a second chance at life by providing financial assistance to animal welfare organizations and rescue groups responsible for the temporary care of animals as they are prepared for adoption into permanent, loving homes. Funding is limited to $2,000 per year. There are also Red Star Emergency Funds. See: www.americanhumane.org/animals/professional-resources/grants/

AMERICAN KENNEL CLUB (AKC)

This division of the American Kennel Club brings together people who love animals by supporting the merits of pet ownership through education, outreach, and grant-making. At present, the fund is accepting applications from women's shelters that permit pets. The awarded grants will provide necessary operational support for the housing of pets or improvements needed in order to house and maintain pets. Eligibility hinges upon the organization's providing of temporary or permanent housing for victims of domestic abuse and their pets, or the pets alone as well as the organization's established relationship with at least one nonprofit shelter for victims or domestic abuse. Multiple types of program grants (Women's shelters, rescues and Hurricane Sandy) each with its own application guidelines, also scholarships. Grants by 501(c)(3) nonprofit organizations submitted by February 15, May 15, August 15 or November 15.

See: akchumanefund.org

AKC SCHOLARSHIPS

The American Kennel Club awards scholarships to college students enrolled in undergraduate or graduate studies that promote responsible pet ownership. For more information, write the AKC Re: John D. Spurling Scholarships for Responsible Pet Ownership, 8051 Areo Corporate Drive, Suite 100, Raleigh, North Carolina 27617.

AKC HUMANE FUND

The Fund awards money to their own AKC Parent Club members as well as non-profit 501(c)(3) organizations which provide rescue and rehabilitation services solely for select breeds of dogs listed on the Fund's current list of registerable breeds. Funds are for operational support and specific projects. Grants amount up to $1,000 per year for up to three years. Grant Applications must be submitted by Parent Clubs with a cover letter on Parent Club letterhead, or by non-Parent Club, 501(c)(3) organizations with a letter of recommendation from a Parent Club on Parent Club letterhead. Submitted applications must include the following materials, in this order: (1) Completed Grant Application form with additional sheets attached as needed to answer questions. Note: The original form is required and must be signed and dated. (2) Financial information regarding your organization, including the most recent financial statements (preferably audited), total current budget for the last completed fiscal year and for the current fiscal year of the organization, and a list detailing the principal sources of ongoing annual support for the organization. (3) Copy of the IRS Determination Letter confirming Section 501(c)(3) status (if applicable). Completed applications must be postmarked by October 31. Mail completed applications to: The AKC Humane Fund, Inc. Attention: Grant Review Committee 260 Madison Avenue New York, NY 10016
See: www.akchumanefund.org/programs

AKC CANINE HEALTH FOUNDATION

The AKC Canine Health Foundation (CHF) awards grants to scientists and professionals in research that concerns the origins of canine illness, diagnosis of canine diseases, developments of effective treatments and the identification of disease prevention strategies. Applications are sought from researchers from a variety of disciplines including, but not limited to, veterinary researchers, geneticists, and molecular biological scientists. Collaborative projects involving investigators from a variety of disciplines and/or institutions, including human health researchers, are encouraged to apply. CHF routinely receives >200 applications/year; therefore, we will continue to ask peer reviewers to screen Special Emphasis grants based on the Abstract page. AKC Canine Health Foundation Requests for proposals (RFPs) are categorized by Research Program Area and grant applications must be submitted in response to specific RFPs.
See: www.akcchf.org/research/application-process/

AMERICAN PET ASSOCIATION SOCIETY FOR THE PROTECTION OF COMPANION ANIMALS (APA SPCA)

The APA SPCA is a national nonprofit that support pets and pet owners in crisis and responsible pet ownership. Funding is available as a grant or loan for pet owners whose pets need emergency assistance or medical /financial assistance. Pet owner applications available at APA Approved Veterinary Facilities. All payments made to the veterinary facility. New program in 2015.
See: www.apaspca.org/PetMed.htm

AMERICAN QUARTER HORSE FOUNDATION

The Foundation provides scholarships to high achieving AQHA or AQHYA members. For more information e-mail foundation@aqha.org.

AMIE'S PLACE FOUNDATION

With an emphasis on New York City, Amie's Place Foundation makes grants to non-profits that provide programs that meet the needs of community members for pet-care assistance during times of crisis. The purpose of these grants is to provide financial support to programs that: (a) provide pet-care assistance to help people through times of medical necessity to ensure they will not sacrifice their own health care needs because of concerns for the well-being of their pets; (b) promote attention to the vital role that responsible companion-animal ownership plays within society and help overcome barriers limiting access to their pets when they most need each other; and (c) support awareness of the unique and healing bond a beloved pet and its human companion share and commitment to help preserve this bond.
See: www.amiesplacefoundation.org

AMPHIBIAN ARK FOUNDATION SEED GRANT

The Foundation's Seed Grant provides funding of up to $5,000 to USA and international individuals, organizations and organizational employees involved in wildlife conservation to support start-up rescue projects for species that cannot currently be saved in the wild. This program supports conservation, research, assessment and education with a mandatory ex situ species component. Deadline of May 1st.
See: http://www.amphibianark.org/about-us/aark-activities/aark-seed-grant/

ANGUS FOUNDATION

Not-for-profit organization to fund and support programs involving education, youth and research in the Angus breed and the agricultural industry. Also Undergraduate/Graduate Student Degree Scholarships for students pursuing a degree in higher education. Range of awards are $1,000 to $5,000. See:
http://www.angusfoundation.org/fdn/ScholarshipsAwards/FdnUndergrad.html

ANIMAL ASSISTANCE FOUNDATION (AAF)

The foundation works to make COLORADO the model state for the care and humane treatment of animals. AAF supports initiatives that 1) promote the spay/neuter of companion animals, both owned and within shelters or rescues, 2) seek to optimize sheltering for companion animals and equines, and, 3) other proposals that are innovative or demonstrate high impact. Funding is aimed at rural communities and those that lack access to resources. Key focus areas are: Overpopulation, Operational optimization. Adoptions & permanent homes, Cruelty prevention and intervention, Innovation and ingenuity, Grants range from $2,000 to $5,000. Larger grants may be made for compelling applications. Applicant organizations must be a 501(c)(3) non-profit organization, a government entity or an entity with a 501(c)(3) organization willing to serve as the group's fiscal sponsor. Email a letter of inquiry first. Spring and fall cycles.
See: www.aaf-fd.org/content/grant-guidelines-2013

ANIMAL CANCER FOUNDATION

The Foundation is a nonprofit organization dedicated to finding a cure for cancer by funding research in and increasing public awareness of comparative oncology. The Foundation provides research grants to medical and veterinary oncology professionals within nonprofit academic research centers WORLDWIDE studying comparative oncology models. Different types of proposals are considered each year. Grants amount up to $50,000. Deadline of January 5th. See website for submission guidelines.
See: www.acfoundation.org/

ANIMAL FARM FOUNDATION

Animal Farm Foundation makes grants to secure equal treatment and opportunity for "pit bull" dogs. All dogs are individuals, and every dog deserves a chance to shine. Four unique grants for non-profit shelters, rescue groups, dog owner/teams can apply for grants typically ranging from $50 to $1,000 – but up to $3,000.
See:
http://www.animalfarmfoundation.org/pages/GRANTS

ANIMAL GUARDIANS

Animal Guardians, Inc. is devoted to the protection and advancement of animals' rights, and the prevention of cruelty to animal accomplished through research, education or charitable work. Awards are made internationally. .Send a letter outlining needs and proposed work to President, Gilbert Michaels, PO Box 1925, Culver City, Ca 90232 Or call 310-204-6600.

ANIMAL WELFARE APPROVED

The Good Husbandry Grants program aims to improve the lives of farm animals through support of farmers within the AWA program as well as those who submit applications. Grants of up to $5,000 will be awarded with an application deadline of October 1st.
See:
http://www.animalwelfareapproved.org/farmers/grants-for-farmers

ANIMAL WELFARE TRUST

Animal Welfare Trust's grant program assists organizations whose work can help alleviate animal suffering and/or raise public consciousness toward giving animals the respect they so need and deserve. Although general organizational funding will be considered, preference will be given to 501(c)(3) organizations with well-defined projects with clear goals and objectives. Areas of priority include farm animal welfare, vegetarianism and humane education that "inform, inspire and educate." Grants will generally be made in the $2,500 to $20,000 range, for a single or multi-year period, though requests on either side of those figures will also be considered. Applicants are encouraged to submit an email inquiry to determine if their project falls within scope of funding. The Trust also awards Student Internships which encourage students to work on projects that facilitate positive reform for animals. Internships must be consistent with The Trust's mission statement.
Send questions to: email@animalwelfaretrust.org
See: www.animalwelfaretrust.org or
http://fdnweb.org/awt/

ANIMAL WELFARE FOUNDATION OF CANADA (AWFC)

The Animal Welfare Foundation of Canada (AWFC) aims to achieve measurable positive change in improving the lives of animals in CANADA, through innovative educational and research initiatives. AWFC fosters an enlightened ethic of animal care. See the website for available grants.
See: http://www.awfc.ca/english/grants.htm

ANIMALS AND ARTISTS

The Foundation gives to animal welfare and wildlife cases, among other pursuits. Grants range in size from $600 to $6,000. Grants are awarded primarily in CALIFORNIA. No applications accepted.
Write: 2714 Carmar Dr Los Angeles, CA 90046

ANNENBERG FOUNDATION

The Foundation funds non-profit programs that work to combat animal endangerment, but emphasize upon organizations within Los Angeles County, CALIFORNIA. Grants range from $10,000 to $100,000. Applications are accepted online year-round though they must be submitted no later than 45 days after their creation.
See:
http://www.annenbergfoundation.org/grantmaking/how-to-apply

ARIZONA HORSE LOVERS FOUNDATION

The Foundation is concerned with the support of all animals, with an emphasis on horses. They provide scholarships for ARIZONA students attending Colorado State University's veterinarian or equine program. The Foundation also helps to fund annual scholarships awarded to students that participate in the Arizona National Livestock Show (ANLS) – deadline March 15.
See: http://csu-cvmbs.colostate.edu/scholarships/Pages/Arizona-Horse-Lovers-Foundation-Scholarship-Endowment-45105.aspx or http://www.anls.org/p/About-ANLS/196

ARMSTRONG MCDONALD FOUNDATION

The foundation will consider only requests for assistance with endangered species reproduction research; for training of guide dogs for the visually impaired; and for training of dogs to be companions for the physically challenged or for mobility restricted seniors. Non-profits in ARIZONA and NEBRASKA may apply. Organizations must appear on a posted pre-approved to submit list. Deadline is by September 15. Download an application.
See:
http://www.armstrongmcdonaldfoundation.org/elig.html

THE AMERICAN SOCIETY FOR THE PREVENTION OF CRUELTY TO ANIMALS (ASPCA)

Founded in 1866, the national animal welfare organization provides local and national leadership in three key areas: caring for pet parents and pets, providing positive outcomes for at-risk animals and serving victims of animal cruelty. Among its funding opportunities are:

ASPCA ANIMAL RELOCATION GRANTS- The ASPCA's Animal Relocation Grants range in size from $1,000 to $5,000 for 501(c)(3) non-profits and public agencies that are dedicated to the safe, humane and efficient relocation of animals to help increase lives saved. Funding is intended to be used for costs associated with animal relocation. Deadline of October 1st.

See: http://www.aspcapro.org/grants

ASPCA PROGRAM-RELATED INVESTMENTS FOR EMERGENCIES AND DISASTERS - The Association provides short-term, low-interest bridge loans to organizations that demonstrate emergency need and the ability to repay within 6-24 months. Funding will be awarded to support animal welfare organizations in cases of natural disasters or economic emergencies. Grants amount from $50,000 to $250,000. Applications accept on a rolling basis while funds are available.

See:
http://www.aspcapro.org/grant/2013/12/11/emergency-and-disaster-program-related-investments

ASPCA ANTI-CRUELTY GRANTS - The Association awards between $500 to $10,000 to USA private, non-profit organizations and public agencies that are dedicated to the prevention and elimination of animal cruelty throughout the UNITED STATES. Funds are intended for costs associated with anti-cruelty efforts.

See: http://www.aspcapro.org/grants

ASPCA EQUINE FUND - The ASPCA Equine Fund provides grants to U.S. nonprofit equine welfare organizations and other animal welfare organizations that care for horses, mules, donkeys and ponies – both wild and domestic – in the effort to protect all equine. Grant ranges from $500 to $4,000 and have a November deadline. The Society also awards grants for general animal welfare and advocacy programs in the United States focused on investigations of cruelty, seizures, vet care, advocacy etc. Typical awards range from $500-$10,000 for relocation, shelter, spay/neuter, emergencies, outreach, training, scholarships and more. Site also includes links to other animal welfare funders and resources. Requests may be submitted online.
See: http://www.aspcapro.org/grants

LIL BUB'S BIG FUND FOR THE ASPCA - This is a new fund (accepting donations to grow the fund) that will award grants to organizations in the UNITED STATES to support cats that need special care or extra help getting adopted due to physical deformity, birth defect, developmental disability, mobility impairment, blindness, deafness, wounds from a disaster, accident or abuse, any permanent disease such as leukemia or diabetes, or just old age. Eligible grant recipients may include, but are not limited to, the following projects that support cats: emergency and ongoing veterinary or medical care, physical and behavioral rehabilitation, hospice and sanctuary care, shelter enrichment, foster programs, adoption events and adoption make-ready costs, relocation programs to improve adoptability, safety net programs for owned cats to reduce pet relinquishment and to keep families together, and costs associated with emergencies, disasters, or cruelty responses.
See: https://www.aspca.org/secure/lilbub

THE AOTEAROA FOUNDATION
The Foundation gives to animal welfare and wildlife causes, among other pursuits. Grants are awarded to pre-selected organizations primarily in Cambridge, MASSACHUSETTS and NEW ZEALAND, so no applications are accepted. Address: 101 Park Ave. New York, NY 10178

AVIVA COMMUNITY FUND
The Fund supports action-oriented ideas from associates of a registered charity that impact communities in CANADA. Grants amount up to $100,000. Submissions accepted until November 24th.
See: http://www.avivacommunityfund.org

THE AWESOME FOUNDATION
The Foundation hopes to create further awesomeness in the universe. Applications for $1,000 micro-grants are accepted on an ongoing, monthly basis. See website for application details.
See: www.awesomefoundation.org

NELL V. BAILEY CHARITABLE TRUST
The Trust supports charitable organizations in Fort Worth, TEXAS for the use and benefit of the state of Texas. The Foundation is administered by the J.P. Morgan is part of JPMorgan Chase & Co. Applications must be submitted online. There is a November 30 deadline.
See:
https://www.jpmorgan.com/pages/jpmorgan/private_ban king/foundations/online_grant_application/search

ELINOR PATTERSON BAKER TRUST FUND
The fund gives grants nationwide for a wide variety of shelter needs, including prevention of cruelty, spay/neuter, shelter improvement and innovative new programs. Four times a year, deadlines not posted. Request $5000 or less. No webpage. Write a brief letter and request required information form/application: Elinor Patterson Baker Trust Fund c/o Nancy Bassett, BNY Mellon Trustee, 10 Mason St Greenwich CT 06830.

HOWARD BAKER FOUNDATION
The foundation supports organizations and individuals whose animal welfare programs help people primarily in southeast MICHIGAN. An application form is not required. Write: 4057 Pioneer Drive Suite 500, Walled Lake, MI 48390.

DR. HILDEGARD H. BALIN CHARITABLE TRUST
The Trust wishes to assist the financially-at-risk and elderly, with a focus on nutritional, legal and medical needs as well as the welfare of dogs who need housing, nutrition, general care and placement within suitable homes. Grants range from $2,500-$20,000. 501(c)(3) organizations located in Santa Barbara County, CALIFORNIA can apply; applications are due by July 31st to be reviewed in October, though submissions are accepted year-round.
See:
https://www.wellsfargo.com/privatefoundationgrants/balin

THE BANFIELD CHARITABLE TRUST (BCT)

Grants made to nonprofit organizations and hospices provide a wide range of pet related programs such as addressing the root causes of pet abandonment, promotion of owner and pet bonding, and work to keep pets with owners. Pet food distribution, veterinary assistance and pet advocacy each have downloadable applications. Pet Peace of Mind® grants are awarded to nonprofit hospice partners. Review guidelines and call 503.922.5801 to discuss project. Funding is also given as Campbell Family Scholarships to undergraduate students pursuing pet related careers.
See: www.banfieldcharitabletrust.org

BANOVICH WILDSCAPES FOUNDATION

The Foundation fosters cooperative efforts to conserve the earth's wildlife and wild places to benefit the wildlife and the people that live there. Unsolicited requests for funds and applications are not accepted.
See: https://johnbanovich.com/wildscapes-foundation/

MARGERY BARKDULL MEMORIAL FUND FOR ANIMAL WELFARE

The Community Foundation for Northern Virginia awards Margery Barkdull Memorial Fund grants to nonprofits that provide animal welfare programs and services in Northern VIRGINIA, including animal rescue programs, shelters and conservation organizations. Grants range in size from $2,000 to $5,000. Applications can be found on the Foundation's website and are available in March with a deadline of April 1st.
See: http://www.cfnova.org/our-programs/barkdull-fund-for-animal-welfare

BARNITZ FUND

The Fund supports religious and charitable purposes including animal welfare organizations in Middletown, OHIO and the surrounding area. Decision dates vary and there are no deadlines. The Foundation is administered by J.P. Morgan, part of JPMorgan Chase & Co. Applications must be submitted online.
See:
https://www.jpmorgan.com/pages/jpmorgan/private_ban king/foundations/online_grant_application/search

EMMA BARNSLEY FOUNDATION

The Foundation provides assistance and scholarships to deserving organizations, individuals, researchers and colleges who wish to prevent cruelty to domestic and wild animals as well as provide preservation, education and study on the subject of animals. Awards usually range from $10,000-$20,000. Applicants must be 501(c)(3) organizations with preference given to TEXAS and NEW YORK.
Submissions are due by the end of August.
See:
http://www.wellsfargo.com/privatefoundationgrants/barn sley

RUTH BARTSCH MEMORIAL TRUST

Supports charitable purposes including funding prevention of cruelty to animals. No geographic restriction. Deadline in September. The Foundation is administered by J.P. Morgan, part of JPMorgan Chase & Co. Applications must be submitted online.
See:
https://www.jpmorgan.com/pages/jpmorgan/private_ban king/foundations/online_grant_application/search

JOSEPH E BEAUCHAMP CHARITABLE TRUST

Supports charitable purposes. Funds prevention of cruelty to animals among other causes. No geographic restriction. Decision in November with an October deadline. Applications must be submitted online.
See:
https://www.jpmorgan.com/pages/jpmorgan/private_ban king/foundations/online_grant_application/search

BEGIN TODAY FOR TOMORROW

The Foundation gives to animal welfare and wildlife causes, among other pursuits. Grants are awarded to pre-selected organizations primarily in CALIFORNIA and NEW YORK, so no applications are accepted.
Write: 501 S. Beverly Dr Floor 3 Beverly Hills, CA 90212

W. & H. BENDER MEMORIAL FUND

The Fund supports charitable purposes and animal welfare organizations among others. OHIO only. Decision dates are in December. Due in November. Applications must be submitted online.
See:
https://www.jpmorgan.com/pages/jpmorgan/private_ban king/foundations/online_grant_application/search

CANDICE BERGEN MALLE CHARITABLE FOUNDATION

The Foundation awards grants to animal welfare and wildlife causes, among other pursuits. Grants range in size from $500 to $50,000. Grants are awarded to pre-selected organizations only, primarily within NEW YORK, NEW YORK and RHODE ISLAND. No applications are accepted.
Write: 529 5th Ave New York, NY 10017

THE BERNICE BARBOUR FOUNDATION, INC.

The Bernice Barbour Foundation was established to fund animal welfare organizations which provide programs to protect, preserve, and nurture companion animals, large animals, native wildlife, and marine species in the United States. Hands on care, animal health/welfare, and veterinary medical research are priorities. Grants for nonprofits range from $500 to $5,000. Grants for universities or veterinary schools for research $5,000 to $20,000. Per instructions and guidelines, the application following accepted format and with all required attachments must be sent paper-based postmarked by the July 31st deadline.
See: http://www.bernicebarbour.org/funding-information.html

BEST FRIENDS ANIMAL SOCIETY®

Best Friends Animal Society's® mission is to bring about a time when there are no more homeless pets. No More Homeless Pets Network member rescue groups and shelters that join and meet certain criteria can apply for grants and scholarships: http://www.bestfriends.org/nmhppartners/. Also, Best Friends have produced a Financial Assistance guide with resources by state.
See: www.bestfriends.org

FRANK STANLEY BEVERIDGE FOUNDATION (BFF)

The BFF exists to fund organizations that serve the common good in Hampden and Hampshire Counties, MASSACHUSETTS. Animal programs are among the many causes supported. February begins new grant cycle. Complete prequalification and application on website.
See: http://www.beveridge.org/

THE GREG BIFFLE FOUNDATION

The Greg Biffle Foundation awards funds to nonprofit humane societies, spay/neuter clinics and no-kill animal shelters that have 501 (c) (3) charitable status in the U.S. Animal welfare groups can apply annually. The deadline during 2014 was August 29. Funding decisions are made in December. Download the guidelines and the application form.
See: http://www.gregbifflefoundation.com

THE BINKY FOUNDATION

The Binky Foundation is a 501 (c) (3) charitable organization dedicated to the protection of domestic and wild animals and the protection and expansion of animal habitats. First Steps grants less than $2,500 are given to bring benefits to organizations in early stages and to help small, local organizations get a firm basis for future sustainability. Forward Steps grants of $2,500 or more help to fund long-term or ongoing projects associated with wild or domesticated animals and protection and or expansion of their habitats. There are two windows for submitting – spring and fall. Download the application forms.
See:
http://www.binkyfoundation.org/binky_foundation_grant s.html

THE BISSELL FOUNDATION

The Bissell Foundation is dedicated to supporting the life-saving efforts of animal shelters and rescues of all sizes across the country and organizations working to reduce the homeless pet population through adoption, spay/neuter programs, micro-chipping, fostering, emergency relief, and hoarding and puppy mill rescue efforts. Download the application from the website.
See: http://www.bissellpetfoundation.org/apply/

ELMER AND MAMDOUHA BOBST FOUNDATION INC.

The Foundation gives primarily to animal welfare causes, among other pursuits. Grants range from $500 to $1,000,000. Grants are awarded to pre-selected organizations in New York, NEW YORK and Beirut, LEBANON, so no applications are accepted.
Write: 70 Washington Sq S New York, NY 10012

THE DAVID BOHNETT FOUNDATION

The David Bohnett Foundation supports animal language research, funding of service animals and eliminating the rare animal trade. The foundation wishes to improve society through social activism. Non-profit organizations may apply through three step process – eligibility, inquiry then responding to invitation to apply. Two rounds in 2015.
See: http://www.bohnettfoundation.org/applications

JOSEPH SLOAN BONSALL AND MARY ANN BONSALL FOUNDATION

Gives grants for general or operating support for Animals/Wildlife programs primarily in Hendersonville, TENNESEE. No deadlines.
Write: Joseph Sloan Bonsall and Mary Ann Bonsall Foundation, c/o S. Gary Spicer, Sr. 16845 Kercheval, Grosse Pointe, MI 48230-1551

LEONARD X. BOSACK AND BETTE M. KRUGER CHARITABLE FOUNDATION

The Foundation funds organizations working on animal welfare and rights issues. Write: Leonard X. Bosack and Bette M. Kruger Charitable Foundation, Inc.
8458 W. Main St. Marshall, VA United States 20115-3231.

HELEN V. BRACH FOUNDATION
The Foundation seeks primarily to prevent cruelty to animals and other causes. Almost all grants awarded in the Midwest, mainly in Chicago, ILLINOIS. $5,000 up to 10% of operating budget. December 31st deadline.
Call: (312) 372-4471 to request guidelines and application form.

OTTO BREMER FOUNDATION
The Foundation gives particular preference to grant-seekers who wish to move their communities forward in meaningful, powerful and broad-based ways. Grants are awarded only to non-profit and government organizations whose beneficiaries are residents of MINNESOTA, NORTH DAKOTA or WISCONSIN, with priority given to local and regional organizations that support Bremer Bank. No deadlines. See website for application details.
See: www.ottobremer.org/grantmaking/grantmaking-overview

THE BRIDGES/LARSON FOUNDATION
The Foundation gives to animal welfare and wildlife causes, among other pursuits. Grants are awarded to pre-selected organizations primarily in CALIFORNIA, so no applications are accepted.
Address: PO Box 3365 Beverly Hills, CA 90212

HOWARD G. BUFFETT FOUNDATION
The Foundation gives to animal welfare and wildlife causes, among other pursuits. Grants range in amount from $600 to $8,000,000. Grants are awarded to pre-selected organizations in GEORGIA, ILLINOIS, MARYLAND, ENGLAND and ITALY, so no applications are accepted.
See: http://www.thehowardgbuffettfoundation.org/

BUILD-A-BEAR FOUNDATION

The Foundation is the philanthropic arm of the Build-A-Bear toy company. The Foundation's Bearemy's Kennel Pals supports animal shelters, organizations that rescue and rehabilitate stray pets, and educational programs about pets in the UNITED STATES and CANADA. One dollar from the sale of each plush animal in this line is donated through the Build-A-Bear Workshop Bear Hugs Foundation primarily to organizations working with or on behalf of domestic pets in areas where the company has stores. Grants $1,000 to $5,000. See:
http://www.buildabear.com/shopping/workshop/Giving%20Back/3100023/10100035

BULKLEY FOUNDATION

Supports charitable animal welfare purposes in CONNECTICUT. Decision dates are in December and deadlines are in November. The Foundation is administered by J.P. Morgan, part of JPMorgan Chase & Co. Applications must be submitted online.
See:
https://www.jpmorgan.com/pages/jpmorgan/private_banking/foundations/online_grant_application/search

THE BULLITT FOUNDATION

The Foundation gives to environmental causes, including animal welfare and wildlife-based pursuits. Grants average around $25,000. Applications are accepted by May 1st and November 1st from the Pacific Northwest region including ALASKA, OREGON, WASHINGTON, IDAHO, MONTANA and BRITISH COLUMBIA. Apply via website.
See: http://bullitt.org/

BURMESTER CHARITABLE TRUST

Supports charitable animal welfare purposes NATIONWIDE. Deadline is May 31st. Applications must be submitted online.See: https://www.jpmorgan.com/pages/jpmorgan/private_ban king/foundations/online_grant_application/search

CARIBBEAN CONSERVATION CORPORATION

The Foundation's Sea Turtle Grants program supports Coastal governments, non-profit organizations, education and research institutions in FLORIDA eligible to receive funding for conservation, education, or research projects that add to the preservation of Florida's marine turtles. Funds may not be used for materials that contain fundraising or membership development language. Grants average in size around $17,000. November deadline. Applications forms can be found on the foundation's website.
See: http://www.helpingseaturtles.org/

CAESAR PUFF FOUNDATION

The Caesar Puff Foundation makes grants for a number of causes including animal welfare. There are no deadlines and no geographic restrictions though most recent awards were in PENNSYLVANIA and WEST VIRGINIA. Interested applicants should send a letter of inquiry to The Caesar Puff Foundation, c/o Beverly Suchenek, c/o Comerica Bank, P.O. Box 75000, Detroit, MI 48275-0001.

T. PATRICK CARR CHARITABLE TRUST
Supports charitable organizations which operate in Tarrant County, TEXAS. Funds animal welfare organizations among others. Decision dates are in September and deadline is July 1. The Foundation is administered by J.P. Morgan, part of JPMorgan Chase & Co. Applications must be submitted online. Or call 214-965-2908 and request an application.
See:
https://www.jpmorgan.com/pages/jpmorgan/private_ban king/foundations/online_grant_application/search

CATS IN CRISIS
The mission of Cats in Crisis is to assist individuals who have exhausted all other financial means to provide the necessary medical care their cat needs. Funds are disbursed directly to veterinarians, pharmacies or animal welfare organizations for services to cats whose owners have financial challenges due to low income, disabilities, etc. Three main causes addressing feline kidney disease, cardiac and mobility issues. Download application. NOTE: Funds were limited in 2014. The website includes a Resources page that includes other funders nationwide that offer Feline Veterinary Financial Assistance.
See: www.catsincrisis.org

CELEBRATE URBAN BIRDS
Each year, Celebrate Urban Birds makes $100 - $750 mini-grants to organizations, educators and youth to help fund creative neighborhood events that introduce the public and youth to birds and incorporate art, greening, science and birding.
See:
http://celebrateurbanbirds.org/community/minigrants/

PHYLLIS & BENNETT CERF FOUNDATION INC.

The Foundation gives to animal welfare and wildlife causes, among other pursuits. Grants are awarded to pre-selected organizations primarily in NEW YORK, so no applications are accepted.
Write: 111 E 80th St Apt 6A New York, NY 10075

THE ROBERTA M. CHILDS CHARITABLE FOUNDATION

The Foundation makes grants for animal/wildlife welfare and protection, animal rehabilitation services for the physically disabled, health care, education, and social services. Giving is focused in MASSACHUSETTS, though inquiries are accepting from organizations in other states. The Foundation has not specified any geographic area of focus. Interested applicants should submit a letter of inquiry. There is no application deadline. The Foundation does not have a website at this time. Write: John R.D. McClintock P.O. Box 639 North Andover, MA 01845-0639 (978) 685-4113

MARJORIE L CHRISTIANSEN FOUNDATION

Supports prevention of cruelty to animals among other charitable purposes in Milwaukee/Racine WISCONSIN. Decisions made in April and October with deadlines in April and October. Submit letter application with nonprofit status attached to the Foundation administers: JPmorgan Chase Bank NA, 111 E Wisconsin Ave 22nd floor, Milwaukee, WI 53201; Call 414.977.2024 for more information.

ROBERT AND LOUISE CLAFLIN FOUNDATION

The Foundation provides grants related to animal health, care and disease prevention within Mason County WEST VIRGINIA among other causes. Projects must be submitted by a 501(c)(3) organization. Write Robert And Louise Claflin Foundation Inc. Po Box 15, Pt Pleasant, WV 25550-0015 or contact Stephen Littlepage at (304) 675-1360

WINIFRED JOHNSON CLIVE FOUNDATION

The Mission is to keep the spirit and passions of Winifred Johnson Clive alive by funding programs and organizations that she supported during her lifetime, and by responding to new organizations that embody and extend her philanthropic heritage. Accordingly, the Winifred Johnson Clive Foundation will fund projects benefiting wildlife conservation and promote the welfare of animals – among other causes. Only Johnson family members (descendants of Grace Phillips Johnson) may contact one of the Foundation Trustees and work with that Trustee to start the grant request process and complete the form required. Matching and collaborative projects are preferred. Contact Fatma Abdullahi, 1660 Bush Street, Suite 300, San Francisco, CA 94109-5308 or Call 415-561-6540.

COLD NOSES FOUNDATION (CNF)

CNF provides funding across the U.S., Canada and beyond for events or programs that offer: Low/no cost medical care, low/no cost spay and neuter, education and rescue wish-list items. Complete an inquiry form. Two windows of opportunity – spring and summer.
See: http://www.coldnosesfoundation.org/grants/

COMMUNITY FOUNDATION OF SOUTHEASTERN ALBERTA

The Foundation awards grants of up to or more than $10,000 to ALBERTA, CANADA non-profit registered charities for projects that will maintain or improve the quality of life for residents of Southeastern Alberta. Funding for animal welfare, among other focus areas. Priority will be given to projects that collaborate and share among agencies. Deadlines of March and September 15th.
See: http://cfsea.ca/grant-recipient-resources/

THE COMPANY OF ANIMALS FUND
Author Michael Rosen (see fidosopher.com) has given out at least $300,000 to animal programs. Priority goes to programs that will help companion animals most, such as low-cost spay/neuter, adoptions, cruelty investigations and rescue. Grants range from $1,000-$5,000. No deadline.
Write: Michael J. Rosen, 1623 Clifton Avenue, Columbus, OH 43203.

GENE CONLEY FOUNDATION
The Foundation awards grants for religious, charitable, scientific, literary or educational purposes as well as for the prevention of cruelty to children or animals. Twenty-eight grants are awarded per year with monetary donations ranging from $2,000-$20,000. Must be a 501(c)(3) organization to apply. Past support has primarily supported North Central TEXAS, but there are no formal geographic restrictions. Applications accepted year-round with a submission deadline of May 1st to be reviewed in July.
See:
https://www.wellsfargo.com/privatefoundationgrants/conley

CONOCOPHILLIPS SPIRIT OF CONSERVATION MIGRATORY BIRD PROGRAM
The SPIRIT of Conservation Migratory Bird Program is a partnership between ConocoPhillips and the National Fish and Wildlife Foundation. The purpose of this partnership is to provide grants in the U.S. and Canada for bird habitat conservation projects in areas where ConocoPhillips has an operating presence. Non-profit 501(c) organizations, educational institutions, and local and State units of governments in ten states can apply. Grants range from $50,000 to $500,000. August pre-proposal and October deadlines.
See:
http://www.nfwf.org/spirit/Pages/2014rfp.aspx#.VDaPcrl0yos

CONSTELLATION ENERGY

The company's Community Champions program awards grants to causes that improve communities. Grants of up to $500 are awarded to non-profit organizations with up to $250 for other community causes. No deadlines.
See: www.constellation.com/community/pages/community-champions.aspx

THE ANNE COX CHAMBERS FOUNDATION INC.

The Foundation gives to animal welfare and wildlife causes, among other pursuits. Grants are awarded to pre-selected organizations primarily in GEORGIA and the greater metropolitan New York, NEW YORK area. Write: PO Box 105720 Atlanta, GA 30348

THE BARBARA COX ANTHONY FOUNDATION

The Foundation gives to animal welfare and wildlife causes, among other pursuits. There are no deadlines and funding is given primarily in HAWAII, with an emphasis on Honolulu. There is no application form required.
Write: 1132 Bishop St Ste 1200 Honolulu, HI 96813

THE RUBY J. CRADDOCK MEMORIAL TRUST

The Ruby J. Craddock Memorial Trust seeks to fund organizations nationwide with a preference for UTAH that support the care and well-being of animals. The Trust distributes nine grants per year that have an average size of $2,500 to $4,500. In total, $60,000 in grant funds are given out each year. Grants are accepted year round with the deadline of October 31st and decisions made in November.
See:
https://www.wellsfargo.com/privatefoundationgrants/craddock

TRAFTON M. & MAUDE W. CRANDALL FOUNDATION

Supports charitable animal welfare purposes nationwide. Deadline is Nov. 1st. The Foundation is administered by J.P. Morgan, part of JPMorgan Chase & Co. Applications must be submitted online.
See:
https://www.jpmorgan.com/pages/jpmorgan/private_ban king/foundations/online_grant_application/search

PETTUS-CROWE FOUNDATION INC.

Supports primarily larger charitable animal welfare advocacy purposes nationwide. Call: 202-483-5866 or Write: 1200 18th Street, NW Suite 801, Washington, DC. 20036-2542.

CULTURE & ANIMALS FOUNDATION (CAF)

CAF takes a distinctive approach to animal advocacy: it is the only all-volunteer organization exclusively dedicated to animal advocacy through intellectual and artistic expression to raise awareness. Individuals can apply via three categories: Research, Creativity and Performance. This organization does not fund "projects" such as animal rescue. Grants range from about $300 to $3,000. Download application. Submit by January 31st deadline.
See: http://cultureandanimals.org/grantprogram.html

THE MARY C. CURRIE FOUNDATION

The Foundation awards 10 grants between $1,000 and $10,000 to organizations dealing with animals and wildlife, among other pursuits. Midland MICHIGAN area. No deadlines. Interested organizations must send a proposal with budget to Mary Currie, 1401 N Parkway, Midland, Michigan 48640 or call (989) 631-3626 for more information.

PROFESSIONAL DAIRY PRODUCERS FOUNDATION

The Foundation supports programs that are consistent with their strategic vision of a professional, proactive and prepared dairy community. They hope to find organizations with unique ideas as to educate consumers about the importance of the dairy industry. Programs and education initiatives focus on either building producer professionalism or maintaining public trust. Grants amount up to $5,000. There are two grant cycles, with application deadlines of December and June 1st. Non-profit organizations within the UNITED STATES are welcome to apply. Applications can be found on the foundation's website.
See: http://www.dairyfoundation.org/grants.php

D.A.S. CHARITABLE FUND- THE PRESERVATION OF FELINE ANIMAL LIFE

The Fund supports organizations that preserve and advance animal life in Lake County, ILLINOIS. Work may include facilitating symbiotic relationships between humans and animals, research initiatives, overpopulation prevention, and animal rehabilitation. Applicants must include their nonprofit IRS determination letter, purpose and planned activity or needs.
See: www.dasfund.com

THEODORE P. DAVIS CHARITABLE TRUST

The Trust supports charitable purposes within the Austin TEXAS Metropolitan Area. Applications must be submitted online. September 15 deadline. See:
https://www.jpmorgan.com/pages/jpmorgan/private_ban king/foundations/online_grant_application/search

DEAN FOODS FOUNDATION

The Foundation, along with partners Professional Dairy Producers Foundation and University of Wisconsin/Madison's The Dairyland Initiative, supports dairy farm communities in the Dallas TEXAS area and those with national focus by helping organizations that provide dairy stewardship educational and development opportunities, with a specific focus on best practices in animal welfare and farm resource management. Letters of Inquiry should be emailed to Dean Foods Foundation at giving@deanfoods.com by March 31 or Sept 30th. Pending availability of funds, applicants that best meet the criteria and further the mission of the Foundation will be invited to complete a grant application April 15 or October 15.See: http://responsibility.deanfoods.com/media/20859/grant_g uidelines_03_05_14.pdf

THE DEBARTOLO FAMILY FOUNDATION

The Foundation awards grants to animal welfare and wildlife causes, among other pursuits. Grants range in amount from $50 to $250,000. There are no deadlines for Community Grants, though they are awarded primarily in the Tampa Bay, FLORIDA area. Application guidelines and procedures can be found on the Foundation's website. See: http://www.debartolofamilyfoundation.com/

THE DEVLIEG FOUNDATION

The DeVlieg Foundation funds nonprofits that focus on wildlife research and encourage respect for and stewardship of the earth. Applicants are often colleges or universities in Southeast MICHIGAN, IDAHO and eastern WASHINGTON. Request an application: 500 Woodward Avenue, Suite 2500, Detroit, MI 48226-5499.

RUSSEL G. & FRIEDA DEYONG FOUNDATION

Funds projects focused on preservation of wildlife. There is no geographic restriction and there are no deadlines. Decision dates are in June and December. The Foundation is administered by J.P. Morgan, part of JPMorgan Chase & Co. Applications must be submitted online.
See:
https://www.jpmorgan.com/pages/jpmorgan/private_banking/foundations/online_grant_application/search

HARRY F. DISE

Funds animal welfare organizations among others in the Prescott, ARIZONA area. . Decision dates are quarterly and there are no deadlines. The Foundation is administered by J.P. Morgan, part of JPMorgan Chase & Co. Applications must be submitted online.
See:
https://www.jpmorgan.com/pages/jpmorgan/private_banking/foundations/online_grant_application/search

DISNEY WILDLIFE CONSERVATION FUND

The Disney Worldwide Conservation Fund (DWCF) provides financial support for the study of wildlife, the protection of habitats, and the development of community conservation and education programs in critical ecosystems around the world. Every year, DWCF awards grants, $25,000 or less, to U.S. nonprofit organizations and their partners abroad. February deadline for Letters of Inquiry. Use the templates posted on the website to prepare the letter and application.
See:
http://thewaltdisneycompany.com/content/conservation-funding

THELMA DOELGER TRUST FOR ANIMALS
The mission of the Thelma Doelger Trust for Animals is to support those organizations in northern CALIFORNIA that effectively and efficiently make better the lives of animals, both wild and domestic, through direct intervention and education. The Trust funds 501(c)(3) non-profits primarily in Northern California and the San Francisco Bay Area. Funding goes to organizations dedicated to the care and maintenance of animals and/or the prevention of cruelty to animals. Applications are accepted year-round and can be submitted online.
See: http://www.thelmadoelgertrustforanimals.org/

DOG AND CAT CANCER FUND
The Fund's mission is to understand, treat and prevent canine and feline cancer and helps to defray the cost of providing malignant cancer treatment for those owners who cannot afford a promising course of treatment due to low income (proof of income is required.) If selected, grants of up to $1,800 are paid directly to the health provider.
See: http://www.dccfund.org/

DOGTIME
The mission of DogTime is to keep dogs out of shelters and in good homes by equipping novice and experienced owners alike with all the information needed to make them, and their dogs, very happy. To show commitment to the rescue effort, DogTime gives back to the animal community through several activities including the DogTime Technology Program ($155 toward website services in order to build awareness, collect donations, etc.), and. the DogTime Annual Grant Program ($500 toward technology solutions) to improve its rescue activities.
See: http://dogtime.com/dog-shelter-grants

DONORS CHOOSE
Teachers submit project ideas to the website and are sponsored by individuals who support their ideas. Amounts given vary and deadlines are open. Ideas can include animal related nature and science projects.
See: www.donorschoose.org

DORIS DAY ANIMAL FOUNDATION
Foundation focuses on spay/neuter programs, special needs programs, senior care programs, medical expenses for senior animals, rescue and placement of senior animals, and pet food pantries; - occasionally funded are grants for senior companion and therapy dogs in hospice situations, training of assistance dogs, wildlife rehabilitation, protective vests for police dogs, education programs, and scholarship in the field of veterinary medicine. Eligible parties are limited to 501(c)(3) non-profit organizations in the U.S.. Applications accepted year-round. Awards rarely exceed $5,000. See website for application details.
See: http://www.dorisdayanimalfoundation.org/

DORIS DAY ANIMAL LEAGUE
The organization is dedicated to reducing the pain and suffering of animals through legislative initiatives, education, and programs to enforce statutes and regulations which have already been enacted protecting animals. Grants range in size from $500 to $700,000. Grants are awarded throughout the UNITED STATES. See website for application details.
See: http://www.ddal.org/

FLORENCE S. DUCEY FOUNDATION

The Foundation supports charitable purposes, mainly in the Houston, TEXAS area. Funds animal welfare organizations among others. Decision dates are in September and deadlines are August 31st. The Foundation is administered by J.P. Morgan, part of JPMorgan Chase & Co. Applications must be submitted online.
See:
https://www.jpmorgan.com/pages/jpmorgan/private_ban king/foundations/online_grant_application/search

ALFRED & LILLIE DUNLAVEY CHARITABLE TRUST

Disbursement of trust income is to be made to further public and private education as well as civic and charitable organizations in Jefferson County, OHIO. Funds animal welfare among other causes. Decision dates are in December and deadline is November 1. The Foundation is administered by J.P. Morgan, part of JPMorgan Chase & Co.. Applications must be submitted online.
See:
https://www.jpmorgan.com/pages/jpmorgan/private_ban king/foundations/online_grant_application/search

THE DALE EARNHARDT FOUNDATION

The Foundation awards grants to animal welfare and wildlife causes, among other pursuits. Grants are given throughout the UNITED STATES with information and application forms available on the Foundation's website.
See: http://www.daleearnhardtinc.com/foundation/

EL PASO COMMUNITY FOUNDATION

The Foundation respond to the needs of non-profit organizations in the greater El Paso, TEXAS region. Human services and the environment are areas of interest, among others. Deadlines of February and August 1st. One animal fund is the James, Janie and Mark Keating Fund.
See: www.epcf.org

THE EMCH FOUNDATION

The Emch Foundation has supported both service dog agencies and animal shelters. Write: The Emch Foundation c/o Foundation Source, 501 Silverside Rd., Ste. 123 Wilmington, DE 19809-1377.

THE EQUUS FOUNDATION

Also known as Horse Charities of America, financial support through the award of grants to charities that are improving the quality of life of horses, using horses to enrich the lives of those in need, and educating the public about the horse's unique ability to empower, teach and heal. Awards of $500 to $5,000 will be given to 501c3 organizations that have been accepted into the Network (apply by March1) and as Messengers (apply by March 31). Grant requests (apply online by May 15) must fall into at least one of two funding priorities: 1) horse rescue, rehabilitation, re-training, adoption, foster care, retirement, 2) providing equine assisted therapies and activities to the public with special needs, including but not limited to those for individuals with physical, cognitive, emotional, behavioral, learning disabilities, life-threatening and/or chronic conditions or illnesses, underserved, underprivileged or "at-risk" youth. Funding toward horse feed/supplements, horse gear/equipment, veterinary/dental/farrier care, scholarships/financial aid, riding apparel/equipment, and small capital improvements.
See: www.equusfoundation.org.

IRENE C. EVANS CHARITY TRUST
The Charity funds various animal welfare, rescue and shelter projects.
Write: Bank of America, NA Co Trustee, 730 15th Street NW, Washington DC 20005-1012 or call 202-442-7328 and request application information.

LEE & GOLDIE EVANS FOUNDATION
Gives to pet causes. Details not known.
Write: Lee & Goldie Evans Foundation for Animals, 1020 Green St.
San Francisco, CA United States 94133-3604

FLORIDA ANIMAL FRIEND INC
Florida Animal Friend is a non-profit organization devoted to helping fund costs of spaying and neutering homeless pets by awarding grants. In the spring of each year, municipal and nonprofit agencies may submit proposals for spay/neuter projects in FLORIDA. Deadline of April 1st. The grant committee will focus attention on those proposals that are the most efficient (more surgeries will be performed for less money) and most targeted (surgeries will be performed on the animals that are most likely to contribute to overpopulation). However, there is recognition that in some areas of the state there may be limited resources for development of low-cost spay/neuter programs and that the cost of providing services in these areas may be higher.
See: http://floridaanimalfriend.org/

FOOD ANIMAL CONCERNS TRUST

The Fund-a-Farmer grants by Food Animal Concerns Trust (FACT) are designed to help U.S. livestock and poultry farmers improve their farm animal welfare. They fund farms specializing in sustainable and humane certifications. Through the Fund-a-Farmer Project, FACT awards grants for projects designed to help farmers (1) transition to pasture-based systems, (2) more generally enrich the conditions in which their farm animals are raised, or (3) improve the marketing of their humanely-raised products. Working, independent family farmers that raise pigs, broiler chickens, laying hens, dairy cows and/or beef cattle are eligible to apply for any of the three types of grants. Projects involving goats and sheep are only eligible for marketing grants. There is an online grant application due by May 1. Grant sizes are up to $2,500.
See: www.fundafarmer.org

FOUND ANIMALS FOUNDATION, INC.

Found Animals offers Michelson Grants of up to $250,000 USD per year for up to three years of funding for research in pursuit of a single-dose, permanent, nonsurgical sterilization product or technology for use in male and female dogs and cats. As a mission-driven and product-focused program, the Michelson Prize & Grants funds research based on merit rather than a fixed approval rate. To qualify for a Michelson Grant, a proposed project must pursue a technology, mechanism, or pathway representing an innovative approach to nonsurgical sterilization. Investigators are encouraged to submit for "proof of concept" studies in cell culture, rodents, and/or target species. The program is open to any entity, academic institutions, biotechnology firms, research institutes, and well-qualified individuals or groups.
See: http://www.michelsonprizeandgrants.org/

FOUNDATION FOR PROTECTION OF ANIMALS

The mission of the Foundation for the Protection of Animals is to promote responsible human interaction with animals for their protection and welfare. During 2012 the focus was on spay/neuter programs in low-income underserved areas of COLORADO, ARIZONA and NEW MEXICO. Spay Colorado program. In addition to providing individual subsidies and referrals to low-income pet owners, still offers sponsorships for targeted spay/neuter events and the trap-neuter-return of feral cat colonies. Low-income clients needing low cost clinic referrals or subsidies may be referred to or whaugen@spaycolorado.org. Inquiries regarding funding spay/neuter events or feral cat colonies also by call 877-654-SPAY. Some scholarships for continuing education to veterinarians and technicians so far as it pertains to high quality/high volume spay/neuter techniques and best practices and sponsorship funds may be available to organizations wishing to hold classes or conferences for the aforementioned purposes.
See: http://protectionofanimals.org/grant-guidelines/

FOUNDATIONS COMMUNITY PARTNERSHIP

The Foundation provides grants to nonprofit human service organizations serving special needs children, youth and families in Bucks County, PENNSYLVANIA. Grants range in amount from $2,5000 to $10,000. Information about the varying grants awarded (with submission deadlines and grant requirements) can be found on the Foundation's website.
See: http://www.fcpartnership.org/

THE REGINA BAUER FRANKENBERG FOUNDATION

The foundation funds animal welfare groups and supports organizations and programs that promote the care, conservation, treatment, well-being and prevention of cruelty to animals. Animal welfare, including efforts to: (1) protect endangered and threatened species by supporting conservation and research; and (2) reduce the homelessness, mistreatment and euthanasia of companion animals by supporting adoption, training, spay/neuter and other programs and by strengthening the capacity of organizations doing this work. No geographic restrictions. July 1 deadline. Applications must be submitted online. Or call (212) 464-2350. See:
https://www.jpmorgan.com/pages/jpmorgan/private_ban king/foundations/online_grant_application/search

LESSER FRANKLIN CHARITABLE TRUST

Support of charities, including animal welfare, in ILLINOIS. Decision dates vary and there are no deadlines. The Foundation is administered by J.P. Morgan, part of JPMorgan Chase & Co. Applications must be submitted online.
See:
https://www.jpmorgan.com/pages/jpmorgan/private_ban king/foundations/online_grant_application/search

ETHEL FRENDS FOUNDATION

The Ethel Frends Foundation supports and promotes canine care and/or canine education in the following CALIFORNIA counties: Los Angeles, Ventura, Santa Barbara, San Luis Obispo, Orange, Riverside, San Bernardino, or San Diego. Apply online. January 15 deadline. Operating support requests are preferred. See:
https://www.bankofamerica.com/philanthropic/foundatio n.go?fnId=112

BIRDIE HARTSOUGH FREY MEMORIAL FUND
The Fund supports charitable purposes in TEXAS. Funds animal welfare causes among others. Decision dates are in September and deadline is July 1. The Foundation is administered by J.P. Morgan, part of JPMorgan Chase & Co. Applications must be submitted online.
See:
https://www.jpmorgan.com/pages/jpmorgan/private_ban king/foundations/online_grant_application/search

THE FULLER FOUNDATION, INC.
The foundation strives to support nonprofit organizations that educate the public, provide shelter, address health, protect habitat, promote interaction with people regarding wildlife, endangered species - their environment, and animals helping people, among other causes in the Boston MASSACHUSETTS area and immediate seacoast area of NEW HAMPSHIRE. Grants range from $3,500-$7,500. Deadlines are January 15th & June 15th Using Massachusetts Common Grant form, submit proposals by mail to John T. Bottomley, Executive Director, The Fuller Foundation, Inc. P.O. Box 479 Rye Beach, NH 03871.
See:
http://www.fullerfoundation.org/FullerFoundation/Home Page.cfm?page=appprocedures

FUND FOR WILD NATURE
The Fund for Wild Nature invests in cutting-edge grassroots organizations and innovative conservation efforts nationwide that meet emerging needs for protecting biodiversity and wilderness; campaigns to save native species and wild ecosystems and threatened wilderness and biological diversity. Online application. Grants typically from $1,000 to $3,000. Deadlines: May 1 & November 1.
See: http://www.fundwildnature.org/proposal-dates-a-guidelines/dates-a-guidelines.html

NATALIE W. FURNISS FOUNDATION

The Foundation supports organizations and humane societies whose goal pertains to preventing cruelty to animals. Six grants are awarded each year with an average size of $3,000. Applicants must be a 501(c)(3) organization. Submissions are accepted year-round, though they must be received by November 1st in order to be reviewed in December.
See:
https://www.wellsfargo.com/privatefoundationgrants/furniss

CHRIS GERMAN MEMORIAL FUND

The Fund supports seven preferred beneficiaries in the ARIZONA and San Francisco area of CALIFORNIA. Funds animal welfare organizations among others. Decision dates are in December and deadlines are the 4th Monday in October. The Foundation is administered by the JPMorgan Chase Bank. Applications must be submitted online.
See:
https://www.jpmorgan.com/pages/jpmorgan/private_banking/foundations/online_grant_application/search

MARY P. GILL CHARITABLE TRUST

Disbursement of trust income is to be applied toward the work and support of named charitable or educational institutions in Louisville, KENTUCKY. Funds animal welfare groups among others. Decision dates are in November and deadlines are October 31st. The Foundation is administered by J.P. Morgan, part of JPMorgan Chase & Co. Applications must be submitted online.See:
https://www.jpmorgan.com/pages/jpmorgan/private_banking/foundations/online_grant_application/search

GLASER PROGRESS FOUNDATION

The Glaser Progress Foundation aims to build a more just, sustainable and humane world. In terms of animal advocacy, they aim to assist humane organizations in combating companion animal overpopulation in the Pacific Northwest. Download the foundation's guidelines before emailing a letter of inquiry. No deadlines.
See:
www.glaserprogress.org/program_areas/animal_advocacy.asp

THE THORNTON S. GLIDE, JR. AND KATRINA D. GLIDE FOUNDATION

This CALIFORNIA foundation's purpose is to support organizations committed to animal protection, agricultural, land preservation and wildlife among other causes. Applications from other states also considered. There are two grant opportunities – one for funding up to $25,000 and one for funding up to $50,000. Does consider requests toward purchase of land; does not consider requests for operating costs. Download application form. Applications accepted between May 15 and August 15.
See: www.glidefoundation.org/grants/

GLOBAL WORKS, INC.

The organization funds animal welfare and wildlife causes, among other pursuits. Grants range in size from $50 to $100,000. There are no deadlines, though funding is given primarily in WASHINGTON DC and VIRGINIA.
Application form not required.
Write: 37 W. 65th St Floor 5 New York, NY 10023

THE GOLDSTOCK FUND

The Goldstock Fund helps rescue organizations or individuals to pay for transportation, boarding, evaluations and medical costs of golden retrievers and golden hearted dogs taken into rescue as well as providing educational information and materials. There are several different funds each with specific funding purposes such as medical care for young dogs with cancer, emergency funds for retrievers with emergency medical issues and more.
See:
http://www.goldstockfund.org/tgf/generalfund_guidelines.html

EDITH J. GOODE RESIDUARY TRUST

The focus is for the prevention of animal cruelty. The grants administrator is Ms. Donna Pease located at 700 Professional Drive, Gaithersburg, Maryland 20879. The webpage is set up as a question and answer system.
See: http://www.goodetrust.org/

EDWARD GOREY CHARITABLE TRUST

The Foundation supports animal welfare and wildlife causes, among other pursuits. Grants are given only to pre-selected organizations with no applications being accepted.
See: http://www.edwardgoreyhouse.org/

EDITH WINTHER GRACE TRUST

Supports prevention of cruelty to animals among other charitable purposes in TEXAS. No deadlines. The Foundation is administered by J.P. Morgan, part of JPMorgan Chase & Co. Deadline August 31. Applications must be submitted online.
See:
https://www.jpmorgan.com/pages/jpmorgan/private_banking/foundations/online_grant_application/search

GREAT LAKES FISHERY TRUST (GLFT)
The Trust provides funding to nonprofit organizations, educational institutions, and government agencies to enhance, protect, and rehabilitate Great Lakes fishery resources. The GLFT pursues its mission and vision through three broad categories: Access to the Great Lakes Fishery, Ecosystem Health and Sustainable Fish Populations, and Great Lakes Stewardship. Deadlines differ based on category.
See: www.glft.org

THE GREYGATES FOUNDATION
The Greygates Foundation is a donor advised fund of the Vancouver Foundation that, among other causes, promotes animal welfare or wildlife preservation. Though funding may be provided for projects in any country, recipient or sponsor organizations must be Canadian Registered Charities. The grant award limit is $3,000 and grants are paid in Canadian dollars. There are no deadlines and grants are only accepted via email.
See: http://www.adminitrustllc.com/the-greygates-foundation/

GREY MUZZLE GRANTS
The organization makes grants exclusively for programs designed to ensure that older dogs get the care and treatment they deserve. Shelters, rescue groups, sanctuaries, and other non-profit organizations should apply. Grants range in amount from $500 to $4,000. During different times, Grey Muzzle may be accepting grants from all areas or only specific areas as well as organizations. Grants are awarded in June.
See: http://www.greymuzzle.org/Grants.aspx

GULF COAST COMMUNITY FOUNDATION

The Foundation invests in the work of effective non-profit organizations that help transform the GULF COAST region through grants and strategic community initiatives. Leveraged grants (greater than $10,000), Transformative grants (greater than $10,000) and Community grants (less than $10,000) will be awarded to address critical needs or opportunities identified as priorities for the region. Varying deadlines. One animal focused fund is the Jack and Trudy Wilson Animal Welfare Fund. See website for application details.
See: www.gulfcoastcf.org

CARROLL J. HAAS FOUNDATION

The Carroll J. Haas Foundation provides funding for animals, preservation and protection, among other causes, mainly in MICHIGAN. Grants are $50,000 or less. Submit a letter of inquiry by December 31.
Write: Carroll J. Haas, 27030 Simpson Road, PO Box 248, Mendon, MI 49072-0248.

SHERRY AND BUDDY HACKETT FAMILY FOUNDATION

The Foundation gives to animal welfare and wildlife sanctuary causes, among other pursuits. Grants range in size from $150,000 to $325,000. Grants are awarded primarily in CALIFORNIA.
Write: 800 N. Whittier Dr Beverly Hills, CA 90210

THE HARDEN FOUNDATION
The Harden Foundation awards grants to 501©(3)
organizations in Monterey County CALIFORNIA for several
causes including Animal Welfare. General support, project
support and one-time capital grant requests are considered
ranging from $5,000 to $100,000. Deadlines are March 1st
and September 1st each year.
See: www.hardenfoundation.org

LYNNE COOPER HARVEY FOUNDATION INC.
The Foundation gives to animal welfare and preservation
causes, among other pursuits. Grants range in size from
$2,000 to $1,000,000. Grants are given to pre-selected
organizations primarily in ILLINOIS and MINNESOTA with
additional funding to WASHINGTON DC and MONTANA.
Applications are not accepted.
Write: 1035 Park Ave River Forest, IL 60305

GUS HAWTHORNE FOUNDATION
The Foundation funds projects in the UNITED STATES that
provide care for both domestic and wild animals in need.
Grants are generally for amounts up to $2,500 and are
awarded to USA non-profit organizations. Deadline in
November.
See:
http://gushawthornefoundation.org/index.php?pr=Guideli
nes

HEART OF GOLD LEGACY FOUNDATION
The Foundation supports causes devoted to helping pets live
healthier lives. Grants are available only to entities
providing rescue of, and shelter for, animals. Grants
awarded average $500. Deadline of September 30th.
Write: 1331 N. Cuyamaca St Ste L El Cajon, CA 92020

DRUE HEINZ TRUST

The Trust funds anti-cruelty causes, among other pursuits. Grants range in size from $1,000 to $600,000. Grants are awarded primarily in NEW YORK and PENNSLYVANIA. Initially, please send a letter requesting application guidelines.
Write: PO Box 185 Pittsburgh, PA 15230

THE JACOB AND TERESE HERSHEY FOUNDATION

The Foundation supports animal welfare and wildlife causes, among other pursuits. Grants range in amount from $100 to $30,000. There is no submission deadline or geographic preference. Applications are evaluated on a case-by-case basis by the Board of Directors. Address letters of inquiry to Terese T Hershey.
Write: 2121 San Felipe Ste. 122 Houston, TX 77019

HEYMANN FOUNDATION

The Heymann Foundation has funded horse rescues, spay and neuter programs, prevention of cruelty of animals as well as other causes. No geographic restrictions. No formal application required. Send proposal with tax exempt information to Heymann Foundation, Board of Directors, P.O. Box 51529, Lafayette, Louisiana 70505-1529 or call (337) 232-4343 for more guidance.

THE HIGH HOPES FOR PETS FOUNDATION

The foundation makes grants up to $500 for animal shelters seeking funding toward food, housing, spay/neuter, capital improvements, training, and educational programs. September deadline.
See: http://highhopesforpets.com/

HIT TWO FOUNDATION
The Foundation awards grants to animal welfare and wildlife causes, among other pursuits. There are no deadlines. Giving primarily in ILLINOIS and OHIO. Applications are accepted, but not required.
Write: 1405 E. Sixth St Cleveland, OH 44114

ROY AND MARIAN HOLLEMAN FOUNDATION
Among the Foundation's preferences are organizations and programs that are devoted to the care, well-being and general welfare of domesticated animals.
Five grants are distributed each year with monetary donations ranging from $10,000 to $25,000. Organizations must be 501(c)(3). Applications are due by the end of September. Apply online.
See: https://www.wellsfargo.com/privatefoundationgrants/holleman

RON AND CHERYL HOWARD FAMILY FOUNDATION
The Foundation provides funding for animal welfare and wildlife causes, among other pursuits. Grants are awarded to pre-selected organizations primarily in CALIFORNIA, CONNECTICUT, WASHINGTON DC and NEW YORK.
Write: 1700 E. Putnam Ave Ste 408 Old Greenwich, CT 06870

HUGS & KISSES ANIMAL FUND
The Fund awards grants to non-profit organizations who wish to provide food, litter, prosthetics, veterinary care, spay-neuter events or help for particular animals in need. Grant limitations are $1,000 and are presented on a rolling basis.
See: http://www.hugsandkissesanimalfund.org/

THE INTERNATIONAL FOUNDATION FOR ETHICAL RESEARCH

The Foundation administers a Graduate Fellowship Program for students who are researching alternatives to the use of animals in science. Fellowships are awarded to candidates whose program of study shows the greatest potential. Any graduate students enrolled in Master's or Ph.D. Programs in the sciences and human or veterinary medicine may apply, though students in other fields of study may also apply. Fellowships provide up to $12,500 annually in stipendiary support and up to $2,500 for supplies per year. The fellowships are renewable annually for up to three years. Continued funding is dependent on student progress and availability of funds. Applications can be found on the Foundation's website.
See: http://www.ifer.org/index.php

ARTHUR L. "BUD" JOHNSON IN MEMORY OF ELAINE V. JOHNSON FOUNDATION

Foundation gives aid to organizations that provide for the care, benefit, support and preservation of Seeing Eye dogs or other trained dogs that assist those with physical impairments. It is also dedicated to preservation of wildlife. The deadline is August 1st but applicants are encouraged to submit a letter of inquiry by May 1st. Grants range from $500 to $100,000.
See: www.aljfoundation.org

CARL W. & CARRIE MAE JOSLYN TRUST

The Trust supports charities benefiting youth, elderly and/or handicapped in El Paso County, COLORADO. Funds animal welfare organizations among others. Decision dates are in December and deadlines are in November. The Foundation is administered by J.P. Morgan, part of JPMorgan Chase & Co. Applications must be submitted online.
See:
https://www.jpmorgan.com/pages/jpmorgan/private_ban king/foundations/online_grant_application/search

JUSTICE FOR ANIMALS FUND

The Justice for Animals Fund provides grants up to $1000 to assist small grassroots organizations in the United States and Canada in animal advocacy and promote animal welfare including vegan advocacy. The Fund does not assist organizations whose main activities are animal rescues, shelters, or spay/neuter programs. There is no deadline and no form. Send a written request with organization's purpose, accomplishments, future plans, overview of grant activity, IRS nonprofit determination letter, Financial Statement or 990, Board Roster including compensation, and organization's literature to: Justice for Animals Fund, c/o Stephen Kaufman, Pres. and Treas. 3200 Morley Rd. Shaker Heights, OH United States 44122.

STELLA M. KEMBLE TRUST

Supports prevention of cruelty to animals among other charitable purposes in TEXAS. Decisions made in November with October 1 deadline. The Foundation is administered by J.P. Morgan, part of JPMorgan Chase & Co. Applications must be submitted online.
See:
https://www.jpmorgan.com/pages/jpmorgan/private_ban king/foundations/online_grant_application/search

A KINDER WORLD FOUNDATION

Supports humane treatment of animals.
Write: David B Schwartz, A Kinder World Foundation, c/o
Ropes & Gray LLP, 800 Boylston Street, Boston MA 02199-
3600

THE KINSMAN FOUNDATION

Native wildlife rehabilitation is the focus and funding is
almost exclusively limited to nonprofits managed by state-
and federally-licensed wildlife rehabilitators that offer
urgent care of injured and orphaned wildlife native to
OREGON and WASHINGTON. A small portion of the
budget is reserved for wildlife appreciation projects or
programs that offer the general public opportunities to
observe and appreciate the natural world.
See: www.kinsmanfoundation.org

THE KIRKPATRICK FOUNDATION

The Kirkpatrick Foundation has a legacy of giving in the
OKLAHOMA City metropolitan area to animal welfare
projects. Nonprofit 501(c)(3) organizations with a solid
infrastructure and at least three years track record of
programming may apply. Younger organizations may
request small grants of $10,000 or less. Use the website's
application checklist, letter of inquiry format and online
system. Call 405.608.0934 or email questions to
pblack@kirkpatrickfoundation.com. The next deadline for a
large-grant Letter of Inquiry is December 1, 2014.
See: http://kirkpatrickfoundation.com/grant-applications

DEAN AND GERDA KOONTZ FOUNDATION

The Foundation gives primarily to animal welfare causes, among other pursuits. Grants range in size from $2,000 to $1,000,000. Grants are awarded only to pre-selected organizations with an emphasis on CALIFORNIA, so no applications are accepted.
Write: PO Box 9529 Newport Beach, CA 92658

KRONKOSKY CHARITABLE FOUNDATION

The Foundation funds 501(c)(3) organizations in TEXAS with an emphasis on cruelty to animals prevention as well as the expansion or improvement of public parks, zoos and wildlife sanctuaries. Proposals are considered on a bi-monthly basis, on odd-number months, starting with January.
See: www.kronkosky.org

ELROY AND TERRY KRUMHOLZ FOUNDATION

The Foundation funds animal welfare projects, among other areas of interest. No grants are given to individuals, with an application deadline of June 30th.
Write: Elroy and Terry Krumholz Foundation, 1430 Broadway, 6th Fl.
New York, NY United States 10018-3308.

JOHN AND MARIA LAFFIN TRUST

Grants awarded to animal welfare organizations or foundations restricted to Los Angeles City or County, CALIFORNIA with a range of $2,000 to $40,000.
Organization goals must include humanely placing shelter animals. Deadlines in May and October.
See:
https://www.wellsfargo.com/privatefoundationgrants/laffin

LATKIN CHARITABLE FOUNDATION

The Foundation awards grants to organizations in Santa Barbara County, CALIFORNIA. To apply for a grant, organizations must submit a letter stating the purpose of their organization and how the grant will be used. Submission deadlines of April and October 1st. Write: 1021 Anacapa Street Santa Barbara, CA 93101

THE AMERICAN LAMB BOARD

The American Lamb Board is an industry-funded research and promotions commodity board that represents all sectors of the American Lamb industry including producers, feeders, seed stock producers, and processors. The Board has two cooperative funding programs available - the Supplier Cooperative Funding Program and the Annual Sponsorship Program. The Supplier Cooperative Funding Program is designed for suppliers to help fund branded retail or food service promotions and help fund local promotions such as festivals, cooking demonstrations and more. A one-on-one cash match is required. Funds are available twice a year in October and April. The Annual Sponsorship Program makes funds available to support events, fairs and festivals with applications due in January.
See: http://www.lambcheckoff.com/programs-activities/

CAROL AND KENT H. LANDSBERG FOUNDATION

The Carol and Kent H. Landsberg Foundation seeks opportunities where a small investment from the Foundation will make a difference in animal welfare and education of people and resources in Southern CALIFORNIA and MICHIGAN as well as few other states. Deadline is August 28 annually; request grants ranging in size from $3,000 to $5,000 for one time costs. Send proposal to Ms. Carol Landsberg, CEO, 701 Ocean Avenue, Suite 303, Santa Monica, CA 90402.

LEAR FAMILY FOUNDATION
The Foundation gives to animal welfare and wildlife causes, among other pursuits. Grants range in size from $200 to $1,000,000. Grants are awarded to pre-selected organizations, primarily in WASHINGTON DC, so no applications are accepted.
See: http://www.normanlear.com/citizenship_philanthropy.html

LEMMON FOUNDATION
The Foundation gives to animal welfare and wildlife causes, among other pursuits. Grants are awarded to pre-selected organizations only, primarily in CALIFORNIA. No applications accepted.
Write: 141 El Camino Dr., Ste 201 Beverly Hills, CA 90212

GRACE B. LUDWIG CHARITABLE TRUST FUND
The Fund supports any charity in Boulder County, COLORADO; grants for capital expenditures and general operating funds considered. Funds animal welfare organizations among others. Decision dates are in January and there are no deadlines. The Foundation is administered by J.P. Morgan, part of JPMorgan Chase & Co. .
Applications must be submitted online.
See:
https://www.jpmorgan.com/pages/jpmorgan/private_banking/foundations/online_grant_application/search

MADDIE'S FUND®
Maddie's Fund® grants are designed to help build a no-kill nation so that all shelter dogs and cats can be guaranteed a loving home. Several different grants ranging from $5,000 to millions go to coalitions, collaborations, universities, government animal control agencies, traditional shelters and adoption guarantee shelters for equipment. No deadlines.
See: http://www.maddiesfund.org/Grant_Giving.html

DAN AND MARGARET MADDOX CHARITABLE FUND

The Fund carries out the vision of its creators by promoting the conservation of wildlife habitat in support of hunting and fishing, in addition to other areas of interest. Applicants must be located in TENNESSEE. Applications due by January 15th.
See:
http://www.maddoxcharitablefund.org/grant_applications eason

WEB MADDOX TRUST

The Trust supports charitable organizations and purposes in Tarrant County, TEXAS that do not receive funding from the United Way. Funds animal welfare organizations, among others. Decision date is in March and there are no deadlines. Applications must be submitted online.
See:
https://www.jpmorgan.com/pages/jpmorgan/private_ban king/foundations/online_grant_application/search

IN MEMORY OF MAGIC (IMOM)

IMOM is an all volunteer 501(c)(3) charity dedicated to making sure that no companion animal has to be euthanized simply because its owner is financially challenged. The organization was named for Magic – a very special cat. Financially challenged cat owners whose cats have a life threatening emergency condition can apply for financial aid.
See: http://www.imom.org/fa/index.htm

MAIN STREET COMMUNITY FOUNDATION

The Foundation welcomes applications from CONNECTICUT 501(c)(3) non-profits serving the communities of Bristol, Burlington, Plainville, Plymouth, Southington and Wolcott with pursuits in animal services, among other areas. Amounts and deadlines vary. Interested organizations must review the General Grant Packet and then contact Jarre Betts, Director of Programs & Community Relations by emailing jarre@mainstreetfoundation.org or calling 860-583-6363 ext. 202 before applying to discuss the proposal and process.
See: http://www.mainstreetfoundation.org/grants-apply.php#cgc

ELIZABETH I. AND LOUIS J. MATT ANIMAL PROTECTION FUND

Distributions provide care and support to animals in need in CONNECTICUT. Grants amount around $5,000 or less.

THE EDWARD W. & AUDREY K. MINK MEMORIAL

FUND at the Main Street Community Foundation in Bristol, CONNECTICUT and surrounding communities provide funds to protect animals.
See: http://www.mainstreetfoundation.org/news-community-impact-matt.php

ANN M. MARTIN FOUNDATION

The Foundation awards grants to animal welfare and wildlife causes, among other pursuits. Grants are given primarily in NEW YORK, with applications not being accepted at this time.
Write: C/O Barkan 60 East 42 Street New York, NY 10165

CHARLOTTE MARTIN FOUNDATION

The Charlotte Martin Foundation is a private, independent foundation dedicated to preserving and protecting wildlife and habitat, among other causes, for groups in WASHINGTON, OREGON, IDAHO, MONTANA, ALASKA. Grants range from $500 to $10,000. January, April & September cycle deadlines
See: http://www.charlottemartin.org/

THE MAPP FAMILY FOUNDATION

The mission of The Mapp Family Foundation is to provide financial resources to qualifying 501(c)(3) organizations, primarily in Baldwin County, ALABAMA, but also in areas of South ALABAMA and MISSISSIPPI. Primary focus is on programs which help people and animals at risk or in need due to unfortunate circumstances, neglect or abuse. No deadlines.
See: http://www.themappfamilyfoundation.org/grant.php

THE LESLIE C. MAPP FOUNDATION

Funds animal welfare organizations, among others. OHIO only. Decision dates are in December and there are no deadlines. The Foundation is administered by J.P. Morgan, part of JPMorgan Chase & Co. Applications must be submitted online.
See:
https://www.jpmorgan.com/pages/jpmorgan/private_ban king/foundations/online_grant_application/search

MASON ANIMAL FOUNDATION

The Mason Foundation for Animal Shelter Design funds needs assessments and schematic architectural drawings for animal shelters in the UNITED STATES who are looking to expand or remodel their building. The initial needs assessment enables animal shelters to initiate a design that ensures their project is optimal for layout, flow and efficiency before the building is constructed. By providing matching grants for a thorough needs assessment, the Mason Foundation for Animal Shelter Design enables shelters across the United States to have this fundamental building block. Grants of up to $4,000 are awarded to public or private animals shelters, as well as rescue groups. Applications can be found on the Foundation's website and are accepted on a rolling basis. Awards are given twice a year.
See: http://masonanimalfoundation.org/

CECIL MAUGER CHARITABLE TRUST

The Trust supports charitable purposes in Licking County, OHIO. Funds animal welfare related organizations among others. Decision dates vary and there are no deadlines. The Foundation is administered by J.P. Morgan, part of JPMorgan Chase & Co. Applications must be submitted online.
See:
https://www.jpmorgan.com/pages/jpmorgan/private_banking/foundations/online_grant_application/search

FLORENCE MAY CANINE RESCUE TRUST

The Trust makes awards to charitable organizations established to aid in the care of neglected dogs, to prevent cruelty to dogs, or to enhance the usefulness of dogs in society. In a proposal letter include the purpose and activities of the grant seeker, the amount desired, how the amount will be used, along with a copy of the IRS determination letter granting tax exempt status. There is a July 1 deadline. Written requests may be submitted to: Edward Hirsch, Trustee C/O Morris, Manninig & Martin Llp, 1600 Atlanta Financial Center, Atlanta, Ga 30326-10443 or Telephone: (404) 504-7686.

WENDY P MCCAW FOUNDATION

The foundation supports a large variety of organizations in Santa Barbara CALIFORNIA and beyond and embodies Wendy's goal to enhance the quality of life for both humans and animals. The foundation has funded rescues, animal centers, and more. Contact the foundation for more information.
See: http://wendy-mccaw.com/philanthropy.html

GEORGE REED MCNEILL ANIMAL WELFARE FUND

Makes funds available to support animal care for low income and general animal welfare largely in Illinois. Write: Paul Galinski, 7000 West 127th Street Palos Heights Il 60463 or call (708) 448-4400

MEACHAM FOUNDATION MEMORIAL C/O AMERICAN HUMANE ASSOCIATION

The Meacham Foundation Memorial Grant was established to provide financial assistance to agencies for shelter expansion or improvements. Only animal sheltering agencies (public or private) and rescue groups are considered for the Grant. Grant money must be used to increase and/or improve the quality of care given to animals. Grants up to $4,000. Funding to any one agency is limited to $4,000 per fiscal year. No deadlines for submissions.
See:
http://www.americanhumane.org/animals/professional-resources/for-shelter-professionals/grant-programs/meacham-foundation.html

MEADOWS FOUNDATION

The Foundation seeks to improve the general welfare of domestic and companion animals in TEXAS regarding cruelty, over population, human-animal connections and best practices. Download forms.
See: www.mfi.org/

MEOW BOW WOW FUND

The Meow Bow Wow fund is truly a fund established to serve as a resource for rescue groups, veterinary based pet orphanages, and the general public to help pay for medical needs such as spay and neuter operations, general check-ups, and many other critical pet needs. Grants range from $500-$1,000. Operated by the all volunteer group WellPetUSA.
See: http://www.wellpet.com/wellpet-foundation.aspx

MELBA BAYERS MEYER CHARITABLE TRUST

One of the Trust's many focus areas in the prevention of cruelty to animals with a particular emphasis on neglected animals. Funding goes to 501(c)(3) organizations with some preference to Pensacola, FLORIDA as well as ALABAMA. Applications accepted year-round with May 1 application deadline. Apply online.
See:
https://www.wellsfargo.com/privatefoundationgrants/meyer2

THE MICCIO FOUNDATION

The Foundation supports projects that address the well-being of animals in IOWA, with primary focus on companion animals but will consider all requests. Funds can be used for, but are not limited to, such projects as humane education, start-up programs, medical care and equipment, spay/neuter programs, caging or adoption support. These projects should have an immediate, direct and measurable effect on improving animal welfare in the target community. Organizations may apply for only one Standard or Mini grant per funding cycle (two cycles annually – May and November). In addition to applying for a Standard or Mini grant, applicants may apply for one Jean M. Walker grant per cycle focused on humane treatment. See:
http://www.miccio.org/

THE CESAR AND ILUSION MILLAN FOUNDATION

The Cesar Millan Foundation believes that a solid pack is a cohesive collaboration. They work with shelters and rescue organizations because together they can create a greater impact. Their programs reflect the work of many dedicated people bonded in an effort to do more to rescue, rehabilitate, and rehome abused and abandoned dogs. The Foundation has many programs for interested non-profits. See website for further details.

See: www.millanfoundation.org

LOUISE TULLER MILLER TRUST

The Trust supports animal welfare organizations, among others, in Metropolitan Detroit and Traverse City, MICHIGAN. Deadlines are in September; decision dates are in April. The Foundation is administered by J.P. Morgan, part of JPMorgan Chase & Co. Applications must be submitted online.

See:
https://www.jpmorgan.com/pages/jpmorgan/private_ban king/foundations/online_grant_application/search

WILMA D. MOLEEN FOUNDATION

Support of charites, including animal welfare, in El Paso, TEXAS. Decision made in the May and the deadline is March 1. The Foundation is administered by J.P. Morgan. Applications must be submitted online.

See:
https://www.jpmorgan.com/pages/jpmorgan/private_ban king/foundations/online_grant_application/search

WILLIAM A. AND ELIZABETH B. MONCRIEF FOUNDATION

The Foundation awards grants to animal welfare and wildlife causes, among other pursuits. Grants range in amount from $300 to $1,000,000. There are no deadlines and giving is primarily in TEXAS. Potential applicants should first send a letter of proposal. Write: 950 Commerce St Forth Worth, TX 76102

MOOR FOUNDATION

Support of charities, including animal welfare, in El Paso, TEXAS. Decision made in the June and the deadline is April 1. The Foundation is administered by J.P. Morgan, part of JPMorgan Chase & Co. Applications must be submitted online.
See:
https://www.jpmorgan.com/pages/jpmorgan/private_banking/foundations/online_grant_application/search

DAVE MORGAN FOUNDATION

The Foundation supports schools or municipalities in Kay County and the Blackwell, OKLAHOMA area. Funds animal welfare organizations among others.
Write: Bill Seymour, PO Box 820, Blackwell, OK 74632

MORRIS ANIMAL FOUNDATION

Morris Animal Foundation helps animals enjoy longer, healthier lives. The Foundation advances health and welfare research that protects, treats and cures companion animals, horses and wildlife worldwide. There are large animal, small animal and wildlife research opportunities and veterinarian student scholar stipends available. Awards up to $50,000. Multiple deadlines.
See: http://www.morrisanimalfoundation.org/

M. EDWARD MORRIS FOUNDATION GRANTS
The Foundation funds organizations nationwide that
support the care and protection of animals. Thirteen grants
are awarded each year with monetary donations ranging
from $1,000-$5,500. Generally, support is given to 501(c)(3)
organizations. Submissions accepted year-round, though in
order to be reviewed in October, submissions should be
received by August 1st.
See:
https://www.wellsfargo.com/privatefoundationgrants/mo
rris

THE MOSBY FOUNDATION
The Mosby Foundation is a 501(c)3 non-profit organization
funded by donations and managed by volunteers which
specializes in paying medical expenses for sick, abused and
neglected dogs. Many of these dogs have been abandoned.
Other dogs have owners with limited means for providing
adequate medical attention for their pets. Completion of an
application requesting financial assistance is
required. Verification of medical need and medical services
is made with the attending veterinary hospital. Each request
is reviewed individually to determine the amount of funding
the applicant could receive. Payment is made directly to the
attending hospital. The Mosby Foundation also offers the
following programs for assistance: Spay/Neuter fund and
Humane Education for elementary schools.
See: http://themosbyfoundation.org/what.html

THE RALPH AND VIRGINIA MULLIN FOUNDATION
The Ralph and Virginia Mullin Foundation makes small
grants up to $2,000 to animal welfare and shelters that are
501(c)3 non-profit organizations or to those striving to
become 501c3's. The deadline is in September. Write: 2401 E
Speedway Boulevard, Tucson AZ 85719 or
email rob@hrtucson.com

THE WANDA MUNTWYLER FOUNDATION

The Foundation makes small grants up to $5000 to ILLINOIS federally tax exempt organizations that prevent cruelty to animals. Project purposes may include promoting the wellbeing of animals; funding animal charities; awarding veterinary scholarships; encouraging the advancement of veterinary education and research into the causes and treatment of animal disease; protecting endangered species or creating open land preserves for wildlife, nature preserves or zoological parks. The deadline is July 31st. Mail applications to: John Pindiak, Vice President, Fifth Third Bank, 640 Pasquinelli Drive, Westmont, IL 60559.
See: http://muntwylerfoundation.org

MUTTNATION FOUNDATION INC.

The Foundation's goal is to end pet suffering and homelessness internationally. The Mutts Across America program was created to provide to support to one shelter in every state. In order to be considered, shelters must run an organization based on high levels of volunteerism, fiscal responsibility, community education, current and modern marketing and advocating spay/neuter/vaccines.
See: https://muttnationfoundation.com/

NATIONAL ANTI-VIVISECTION SOCIETY'S SANCTUARY FUND

Grants of up to $5,000 support animal shelters and rescue groups' emergency-intervention efforts on behalf of animals who are neglected or abused, including the cost of food, transportation, and veterinary care. Nonprofit 501(c)(3) organizations may apply.
See: http://www.navs.org/donate/sanctuary-fund-overview

NATIONAL DAIRY SHRINE

Annual scholarship awards named for journalist Marshall E. McCullough are given out to college bound students who plan a career in dairy journalism. For more information, email info@dairyshrine.org.

NATIONAL FISH AND WILDLIFE FOUNDATION (NFWF)

NFWF provides funding on a competitive basis to projects in the U.S. and Canada that sustain, restore, and enhance fish, wildlife, and plants and their habitats. From herring, trout and coho to turtles, cottontails and sea birds, NFWF works to conserve more than 50 distinct species and wildlife habitats; each opportunity has a description of the grant goals, strategies and its application process. Some grants begin with a business plan or discussion with NFWF staff representatives; others have request for proposal dates. See:
http://www.nfwf.org/whatwedo/grants/Pages/home.aspx#.VDaR27l0yos

NATIONAL SHEEP INDUSTRY IMPROVEMENT CENTER (NSIIC)

The mission of the NSIIC is to assist the U.S. Sheep and Goat Industries by strengthening and enhancing the production and marketing of sheep, goats, and their products. The NSIIC has the flexibility to deliver financial assistance to the sheep and goat industries through a number of different methods including grant and a low interest loan programs. For more information about the NSIIC operations, programs and how to complete an application, visit the webpage. See: www.nsiic.org

NESTLE PURINA PETCARE

Charitable grants are generally given to established pet-related organizations for fundraising or responsible pet ownership programs. Small grants may be requested for capital campaigns and education programs. Applications are accepted from the greater St. Louis area and the cities where manufacturing facilities are operated: Allentown, PA; Atlanta, GA; Bloomfield, MO; Cape Girardeau, MO; Clinton, IA; Crete, NE; Davenport, IA; Denver, CO; Dunkirk, NY; Flagstaff, AZ; Fort Dodge, IA; Hager City, WI; Jefferson, WI; King William, VA; Maricopa, CA; Mechanicsburg, PA; Oklahoma City, OK; Springfield, MO; St. Joseph, MO; Weirton, WV; Zanesville, OH.
See: https://www.purina.com/better-with-pets/pet-welfare or catcow.com

RYAN NEWMAN FOUNDATION

The Foundation funds organizations focused on low cost spay/neuter clinics and encouraging people to adopt from animal shelters, in addition to educating people on the importance of conservation. Applicants must be 501(c)(3) organizations and funding must be used to help shelters and families sterilize and vaccinate dogs and cats.
See: http://www.rescueranch.com/services

DON NIERLING MEMORIAL FOUNDATION

The Foundation supports general charitable purposes in ARIZONA and NORTH DAKOTA. Funds animal welfare organizations among others. Decision dates are quarterly and there are no deadlines. The Foundation is administered by J.P. Morgan, part of JPMorgan Chase & Co. Applications must be submitted online.
See:
https://www.jpmorgan.com/pages/jpmorgan/private_ban king/foundations/online_grant_application/search

THE LAURA J. NILES FOUNDATION

The Laura J. Niles Foundation encourages and supports
charitable initiatives that foster life enrichment through
canine and other types of animal companionship. The
Foundation is seeking ways to benefit animals, particularly
dogs, and is especially interested in efforts that help animals
and people simultaneously. Target areas that include specific
medical research, animal adoption, search & rescue,
assistance dogs, and similar fields of interest. Non-profit
organizations nationwide, mostly in the northeastern U.S.,
may apply for grants $2,000-$50,000. No deadlines. Email:
AGaran@fcsn.com to request an application form.
See: www.ljniles.org

MARIA NORBURY FOUNDATION

Grants awarded across the U.S. and internationally for spay-
neuter clinics, educational events, animal protection efforts.
May not be receptive to unsolicited requests. For more
information, write Maria Norbury Foundation, P.O. Box 8,
Leavenworth, Washington 98826

NORCROSS WILDLIFE FOUNDATION

To apply for a grant from the Norcross Wildlife Foundation,
applicants must be non-profit organizations as determined
by the IRS. Norcross makes Restricted Grants only; for
program-related office and field equipment and materials
and public-education materials. The Foundation supports a
very limited amount of community-service work, confined
to the NEW YORK CITY Metro area and the towns near the
Norcross Wildlife Sanctuary. Norcross will consider requests
for no more than $10,000; but please note that grants average
less than $5,000. See submission information on their
website. No deadlines.
See: http://www.norcrossws.org/

NORTH CAROLINA VETERINARY MEDICAL ASSOCIATION

The NCVMA is a professional organization of veterinarians dedicated to compassionate animal care and quality medicine. In addition to promoting integrity and excellence in veterinary medicine, continuing education programs and conferences, and supporting its members, it also gives Animal Welfare Grants to public and private shelters needing financial assistance for supplies or improvements to animal housing facilities in NORTH CAROLINA. Grants amount up to $5,000. Rolling application deadlines. For more information, call (800) 446-2862 or (919) 851-5850 or See: http://www.ncvma.org/ or http://www.ciclt.net/sn/clt/ncvma/default.aspx?ClientCode=ncvma

THE NOVOGRATZ-CACERES FAMILY FOUNDATION

The Foundation awards grants to animal welfare and wildlife causes, among other pursuits. Grants range in amount from $1,000 to $1,000,000. Grants are given to pre-selected organizations only, primarily in New York, NEW YORK.
Write: 100 Wall St 11th Floor New York, NY 10005

THE ONYX & BREEZY FOUNDATION

The Onyx & Breezy Foundation makes grants to help pets get necessary medical treatment by veterinarians. A complete grant application includes the questionnaire, financials and more.
See: www.onyxandbreezy.org

OXBOW ANIMAL HEALTH

Oxbow Animal Health makes grants to rescue organizations, foster networks, humane societies, wildlife rehabilitation groups, sanctuaries and specialty organizations in the U.S. and CANADA that find permanent homes for small animals and work to rehabilitate wildlife. Funding is provided for education or outreach, capital improvements, and operating support. Applications must be postmarked between June 1 and August 31. Download application. Scholarships also available for students seeking companion animal welfare related careers.
See: www.oxbowanimalhealth.com

FRANCES HOLLIS PALMROS TRUST

The Trust supports charitable purposes in Fort Worth, TEXAS. Funds animal welfare related organizations among others. Decision date is in June and the deadline is February 28. Online Application. See:
https://www.jpmorgan.com/pages/jpmorgan/private_ban king/foundations/online_grant_application/search

WILLIAM AND CHARLOTTE PARKS FOUNDATION FOR ANIMAL WELFARE

The Foundation was established to improve the status of animals worldwide through studies of the science and philosophy of animal welfare/rights and to reduce, through practical efforts and initiatives, the suffering and harm inflicted on animals by human beings. Grants are made to organizational or institutional projects, grassroots activities, or academic studies that promise to advance animal welfare or for specific projects - Capital, Project, and General Operating grants that benefit animals. Grants are made to non-profit organizations in amounts up to $10,000. Apply online. Applications accepted from February 1st thru May 1st.
See: http://www.parksfoundation.org/

PARSEMUS FOUNDATION

The Parsemus Foundation only supports research which meets the new European standards for animal care, which are much more stringent than the current American standards. All foundation-funded projects are required to meet or exceed these standards, or, in field-based rather than laboratory-based research, to improve the lives of the animals studied consistent with the spirit of these standards. More information on requirements for grant-making can be found on the foundation's website.
See: http://www.parsemusfoundation.org/

CLAYTON AND CAROL PAUL FUND FOR ANIMAL WELFARE

The Fund within the Community Foundation of Central Georgia provides monetary grants to Central GEORGIA (1) animal humane societies, (2) animal shelters, (3) animal adoption agencies, (4) low-cost spay-neuter clinics, (5) wildlife rehabilitators, (6) as well as other animal welfare organizations, in order to allow these volunteer organizations to use their enormous enthusiasm, drive and willingness to reduce animal suffering and homelessness. Grant amounts are usually less than $2,000. Deadlines: - June 30th and December 31st.
See: http://www.cfcga.org or http://www.cfcga.org/page.aspx?pid=668.

THE PAULUS FOUNDATION, INC.

The Paulus Foundation, Inc. is an independent foundation providing general and operating support for animal welfare and human services. Giving is on a national basis. The foundation gives to pre-selected organizations only.
Write: Sophie J. Alweis, Vice President 21447 Waterford Place West Linn, OR 97068 or call 503-657-4706

PEDIGREE FOUNDATION GRANTS

The Foundation's mission is to help dogs by providing grants to 501(c)(3) nonprofits, shelters and rescue groups — and by encouraging dog adoption. Innovation Grants range in amount from $10,000-$25,000 and are awarded to organizations who aim to increase dog adoptions while Operation Grants provide $1,000 donations to animal shelters who promote the same. Works in partnership with the Petfinder Foundation.

See: http://www.pedigreefoundation.org/

PEGASUS FOUNDATION

The Pegasus Foundation focuses its support of companion animal programs on spay-neuter services and humane education in several regions, including Cape Cod, MASSACHUSETTS; Southeast FLORIDA; Native American lands in southwestern United States; and the islands of the Caribbean. Past awards $2,000-$10,000.

See: http://www.pegasusfoundation.org

PET CARE TRUST

Kids benefit from exposure to pets in the classroom in ways that help to shape their lives for years to come. The program's goal is to establish healthy child-pet relationships at an early age by supporting responsible pet care in elementary and middle school classrooms across the country. Awards are available to preschool through 8th grade teachers in U.S. to purchase small animals and reptiles at a Petco or Petsmart store. Half off purchase vouchers and also sustaining grants for pet food or supplies.

See:
https://netforum.avectra.com/eWeb/StartPage.aspx?Site=PCT or
http://www.petsintheclassroom.org

PETCO FOUNDATION

The Foundation funds nonprofit organizations, municipal/governmental agencies and educational institutions involved in animal causes in the United States. Applications are accepted year-round. The opportunities (adoption, rescue, disaster relief, education, spay/neuter clinics, etc.) change depending on the charitable partners. There are spring and summer windows for submitting applications.

For more information See: http://www.petcofoundation.org
To create an account and apply, See:
https://www.grantinterface.com/Common/LogOn.aspx?eq
s=B-6LQaKoie34djerIzPnqQ2.

FOLKE H. PETERSON FOUNDATION

The mission of the Folke H. Peterson Foundation is to prevent cruelty to animals and to benefit and improve the quality of life for animals across the U.S. by awarding grants $5,000 to $20,000 to protect animals, secure medical assistance or food. No organizations that euthanize animals are eligible. The deadline in 2014 was October 31. There is an online application with guidelines.

See: fdnweb.org/peterson/application/

PETFINDER FOUNDATION

The public charity works to end the euthanasia of adoptable pets by assisting animal shelters and rescue groups across NORTH AMERICA. Become a Petfinder member to be eligible for grant opportunities that help to prepare for and recover from disaster, vaccinate and spay or neuter pets in care, purchase toys or beds for a shelter, and more. Opportunities vary with various sponsors. One program called Cats R Cool developed in partnership with the animal rescue site GreaterGood.org supported cat castles

See: www.petfinderfoundation.com.

PET FOOD DIRECT

Donations requested by nonprofit organizations are considered by sending an email to donations@pet360.com with Donation Request in the subject line. Some sanctuaries, rescues and shelters have benefited from the PFD Rewards Program with donated meals. Send request to same email with PFD Rewards Program in subject line of email. For each email, include official name of organization, Tax ID number, 501(c)3 letter and contact information.
See: www.petfooddirect.com

PETSMART CHARITIES GRANT PROGRAM

PetSmart Charities® and PetSmart Charities of Canada® are nonprofit animal welfare organizations that save the lives of homeless pets. PetSmart Charities Grant Programs provides limited financial assistance to fund innovative programs, with measurable results, that help accomplish its mission to improve the quality of life for all companion animals through programs that save the lives of homeless pets and promote healthy relationships between people and pets. Non-profit animal welfare organizations, municipal animal control facilities and educational establishments in U.S. and CANADA interested in spay/neuter programs should apply. No geographic restrictions. No deadlines. Note: See: http://www.petsmartcharities.org/pro/grants/spay-neuter

PLANET DOG FOUNDATION

From the earliest days of Planet Dog, the founders were committed to creating a national grant program to make maximum impact with limited resources. The goal is to fund programs that train, place and support dogs helping people in need. Funding is allocated nationwide to promote and financially support service-oriented canine programs such as assistance dogs, therapy dogs, search and rescue programs or police, fire and military dogs. Grants usually less than $7,500. No deadlines.
See: http://www.planetdogfoundation.org/grantmaking.aspx

POLLOCK COMPANY FOUNDATION and POLLOCK PERSONAL FOUNDATION

Supports charitable purposes and funds animal welfare organizations among others. OHIO only. Decision dates are in December and deadline is in November. The Foundation is administered by J.P. Morgan, part of JPMorgan Chase & Co. Applications must be submitted online.See: https://www.jpmorgan.com/pages/jpmorgan/private_ban king/foundations/online_grant_application/search

LEO POTISHMAN FOUNDATION

The Foundation supports charitable purposes with preference to Fort Worth, TEXAS. Funds animal welfare organizations among others. Decision date is in June and deadline is February 28. The Foundation is administered by J.P. Morgan, part of JPMorgan Chase & Co. Applications must be submitted online.
See:
https://www.jpmorgan.com/pages/jpmorgan/private_ban king/foundations/online_grant_application/search

MARY J. PROCTOR
Supports charities that benefit children in the Indianapolis,
INDIANA area and funds animal welfare organizations
among others.. Decision dates are in October and the
deadline is in September. Applications must be submitted
online.
See:
https://www.jpmorgan.com/pages/jpmorgan/private_ban
king/foundations/online_grant_application/search

PROJECT PAWSITIVE
The Foundation provides extreme makeovers for animal
shelters in need within the UNITED STATES. There are no
application deadline, but the Foundation is only able to fund
around 4 shelters each year. Applications can be found on
the Foundation's website.
See: http://www.projectpawsitive.com/

PRYOR'S PLANET
The mission is to help grassroots efforts in saving lives,
providing sanctuary and making the world a better place for
all creatures.
See: http://www.pryorsplanet.com/

NINA MASON PULLIAM CHARITABLE TRUST
The Trust accepts requests from only charitable
organizations located in and serving the metropolitan areas
of Indianapolis, INDIANA and Phoenix, ARIZONA. The
Trust seeks to protect animals and nature among other
pursuits and provide humane and wellness services for
domestic animals including shelter, rescue and adoption.
Grants range from $10,000-$75,000 submitted via the
website. Grants are reviewed in February and August.
See: http://www.ninapulliamtrust.org/

LILA D. RANKIN TRUST

The Trust supports charitable, scientific, literary or education purposes, including the prevention of cruelty to animals in Fort Madison, IOWA area. Funds animal welfare organizations among others. Decision dates are in November and deadlines are in October. The Foundation is administered by J.P. Morgan. Applications must be submitted online. See: https://www.jpmorgan.com/pages/jpmorgan/private_ban king/foundations/online_grant_application/search

REDROVER

Formerly called LifeLine Grants, RedRover Relief grants help provide financial assistance grants so pet owners, Good Samaritans and rescuers can care for animals who need urgent veterinary care as well as providing emergency shelter organizations with the ability to keep victims of domestic violence united with their pets during times of crisis. Download the Relief grant's guidelines. The typical grant is $100 to $200, however larger grants may be awarded based upon several factors, including: medical urgency, financial need, available funding and eligibility. The Domestic Violence Safe Housing grants award up to $3,000 each to as many as eight emergency shelter organizations to create space for the pets of domestic violence victims to be temporarily housed. At least one pet must be able to be housed after the grant's acceptance and the project's completion. Only 501 (c)(3) nonprofits can apply. See: http://www.redrover.org/node/1491

THE JOHN S AND CYNTHIA REED FOUNDATION
The Foundation gives to animal welfare and wildlife causes, among other pursuits. Grants range in size from $5,000 to $2,400,000. Grants are awarded primarily in NEW YORK, NEW JERSEY and MASSACHUSETTS with no applications being accepted.
Write: PO Box 803878 Chicago, IL 60680

REMY FUND
Ken Jackson established the Remy Fund, a special Field of Interest Fund of the Community Foundation of Greater Birmingham, ALABAMA, named for his late dog, Remy. Remy Fund grants support nonprofit organizations that work with traditional companion animals such as dogs, cats and horses. Grant applications for rescue/shelter programs, spay/neuter programs, animal assisted therapy programs, education and advocacy programs and service dog programs.
See: www.foundationbirmingham.org.

RESCUE BANK
This organization donates pet food that the manufacturer can no longer sell to less visible shelters in need. The shelters are then able to put the savings from thief food budget towards spay/neuter programs. Shelters must be pre-qualified and non-profit in order to apply.
See: http://www.rescuebank.org/

RHODE ISLAND VETERINARY MEDICAL ASSOCIATION (RIVMA) COMPANION ANIMAL FOUNDATION

The RIVMA Companion Animal Foundation is to make compassionate veterinary care available to all pets by funding the cost of treatment for the sick and injured pets of low-income owners in RHODE ISLAND. There is an eligibility step. There is a separate application for seeking discounts for spay and neutering costs.
Contact caf@hannahstreet.com or See:
.www.companionanimalfoundation.org.

RIDENOUR ENDOWMENT FUND

Supports charitable work in Flushing, NEW YORK area. Funds animal welfare organizations among others. Decision dates are in November and deadlines are in October. The Foundation is administered by J.P. Morgan. Applications must be submitted online. See:
https://www.jpmorgan.com/pages/jpmorgan/private_ban king/foundations/online_grant_application/search

R M S M FOUNDATION

The Foundation supports organizations in INDIANA animal welfare organizations among others. Decision dates are quarterly and there are no deadlines. Applications must be submitted online. Support typically $5000 or less. See:
https://www.jpmorgan.com/pages/jpmorgan/private_ban king/foundations/online_grant_application/search

THE ROBERTS FOUNDATION
The Foundation gives to animal welfare and wildlife causes, among other pursuits. Grants range in size from $100 to $3,000,000. Grants are awarded in Northern CALIFORNIA, emphasis on San Francisco, San Mateo, Sonoma, Santa Clara and San Benito counties. Applications are closed.
See: http://redf.org/

ROOM TO RUN™
Funded by the Nutro Company, grants are available to fund enhancement efforts in public, non-profit dog parks serving local U.S. Communities.
See: www.easymatch.com/NutroRoomToRun

ROSES FUND FOR ANIMALS
When there is a situation where the pet or found animal has a good chance of being well with veterinarian care, but the owner or a Good Samaritan can't afford it; Rose's Fund will try to help cover the cost. The veterinarian will call the fund after the owner has used his/her own resources and applied for a "care card" at the veterinarian's office. Case by case funding assistance is determined, the pet has a life-threatening illness, injury or condition, the condition requires immediate or prompt veterinary intervention in order for the pet/found animal to survive, the veterinarian's prognosis indicate a positive outcome. Read the guidelines and download the application. For more information call: 877-505-4234
See: http://www.rosesfund.org/

SCAIFE FAMILY FOUNDATION

Grant awards support and develop programs that promote animal welfare, and that demonstrate the beneficial interaction between humans and animals. Grant requests should be in letter form signed by the organization's President, and have the approval of the organization's Board of Directors. The letter should include a concise description of the specific program for which funds are requested. Also attach a budget for the program and for the organization, a list of the Board of Directors, a copy of the organization's tax exemption under Section 501 (c)(3) and a copy of the most recent 990 filed with the IRS. Also, if available, their latest audited financial statement and annual report. No deadlines but requests for the spring meeting should be received by March 1st and September 1st for the fall meeting. Send grant application letter and package to: Mr. David A Zywiec, President, Scaife Family Foundation, 777 South Flagler Drive West Tower, Suite 903, West Palm Beach, Florida 33401

KENNETH A. SCOTT CHARITABLE TRUST

The Trust supports organizations in OHIO, MICHIGAN and a few other Great Lake states that care and protect animals. Also awards for homeless companion pets, spay/neuter programs, wellness, behavior training, etc. Awards range from $1,000 to over $50,000. Deadlines are March 15 & September 15 for Ohio organizations and June 15 & December 15 annually for national or other Great Lakes organizations.
See: http://kennethscottcharitabletrust.org/

ALBERT SCHWEITZER ANIMAL WELFARE FUND
The Fund was named for the famed scientist and humanitarian in recognition of his philosophy of Reverence for Life. The fund supports many types of projects in the United States: Humane education, materials and media presentations; Seeking and implementing humane solutions to the problem of pet overpopulation; Enhancing the humaneness and efficiency of animal shelter operations; Protecting wild animals; Assisting protection of animals used for food or for elimination of such use; Discovering ways to eliminate pain and suffering of animals used in biomedical research and testing, through reduction of numbers of improved protocols or by use of non-sentient substitutes. Grants are $5,000 or less. Decisions made in April and October. Download form and instructions. Submit electronically or paper based.
See: www.schweitzerfund.org/

JOHN J & MARY R SCHIFF FOUNDATION
The Foundation gives to animal welfare and wildlife causes, among other pursuits. Grants range in size from $5,000 to $1,800,000. Grants are given to pre-selected organizations with an emphasis on Cincinnati, OHIO. No applications are accepted.
Write: PO Box 145496 Cincinnati, OH 45250

WEBER W SEBALD FOUNDATION
Supports charitable purposes. Funds animal welfare organizations among others. OHIO only. Decision dates and deadlines vary. Applications must be submitted online.
See: https://www.jpmorgan.com/pages/jpmorgan/private _banking/foundations/online_grant_application/search

THE ELMINA B. SEWALL FOUNDATION

The Elmina B. Sewall Foundation's supports animal welfare organizations working in MAINE to build capacity and to address the common issue of unwanted cats facing communities and animal shelters around the state. Unwanted Cat Population grants support spay/neuter programs, education, capacity building for animal shelters and other mechanisms. Capacity Building Grants support efforts that will have significant, measurable impact on organizations' ability to perform their work - including leadership development; improved sheltering, management and governance practices; and fundraising sophistication - are of particular interest. Grants are due June 15; the online application is available from March 15 to June 15. Contact the Elmina B. Sewall Foundation, 15 Main Street, Suite 230, Freeport, ME 04032, (207) 865-3810 or info@sewallfoundation.org. See www.sewallfoundation.org

THE SEVENTH GENERATION, INC.

The Seventh Generation, Inc. Corporate Giving Program makes charitable contributions to nonprofit organizations involved with the environment, animals, and health. Support is given on a national basis with an emphasis on VERMONT, including within a 50-mile radius of Burlington; giving also to regional and national organizations. The foundation provides: donated products, employee volunteer services, general/operating support, public relations services, and sponsorships. Interested applicants should submit the following in an e-mail proposal: Contact person, Name, address and phone number of organization. Detailed description of project and amount of funding requested. There is no deadline. Final notification will be given within three to four weeks. See:
http://www.seventhgeneration.com/responsibility/foundation

SHOUP FOUNDATION
The Foundation funds animal welfare organizations among other causes in COLORADO; north of Denver. Decision dates are in June and deadlines are in May. The Foundation is administered by J.P. Morgan, part of JPMorgan Chase & Co. Applications must be submitted online.
See: https://www.jpmorgan.com/pages/jpmorgan/private _banking/foundations/online_grant_application/search

SHUMAKER FAMILY FOUNDATION
Among the foundation's areas of interest is environmental justice, which includes animal rights. The organization funds non-profit organizations and those with a non-profit serving as its fiscal agent, primarily in Kansas City bi-state area, though animal rights projects can be funded anywhere where trustees can travel for a site visit. Download application form. There is a March 15th deadline.
See:
http://www.shumakerfamilyfoundation.org/wordpress/

SIEGFRIED & ROY FOUNDATION, INC.
The Foundation's SARMOTI Foundation is dedicated to protecting, conserving and preserving endangered and threatened animals globally, with particular focus on the big cats: tigers, lions, cheetahs, panthers and leopards. Grants are awarded to pre-selected organizations, primarily in NEVADA and CALIFORNIA. No applications are accepted.
See: http://siegfriedandroy.com/?page_id=85

THE SAM SIMON FOUNDATION

The Foundation's goal is to provide neutering and spaying services for cats and dogs. Giving also goes towards training dogs to assist hearing-impaired individuals and veterans. Grants are awarded to pre-selected organizations only, with an emphasis on CALIFORNIA. No applications accepted.
See: http://www.samsimonfoundation.com/

BOBBYE AND JERRY SLOAN HAND-IN-HAND FOUNDATION, INC.

The Foundation awards grants to animal welfare and wildlife causes, among other pursuits. Grants range in size from $250 to $50,000. Grants are awarded throughout the UNITED STATES.
Write: 6043 N. Milwaukee Ave C/O Brian K. Sloan Chicago, IL 60646

SNYDER FOUNDATION FOR ANIMALS

The organizations funds humane organizations and wishes to promote the humane treatment of animals through education and philanthropic support by working with nonprofits in MARYLAND. Interest includes: Spay/neuter programs; pet overpopulation; adoption of shelter animals; rescue of abused animals; medical treatment for shelter animals; wildlife support and rehabilitation; helping low income owners keep their pets, and other like projects designed to promote the welfare of animals. Grants are less than $10,000. Deadline is April 30th. Nonprofits may wish to first call 410-366-0787.
See: http://www.snyderanimals.org/grants.html

THE IAN SOMERHALDER FOUNDATION (ISF)

The ISF, launched by the actor Ian Somerhalder, has an eco focus which includes providing funds for sick and injured homeless animals in the U.S. and CANADA. The ISF Emergency Medical Care Grant for Animals provides financial assistance up to $2,500 to animal welfare organizations, agencies, and in some cases individual rescuers, responsible for the care of animals recovering from abuse, neglect or injuries suffered from a traumatic event and give animal victims a second chance by alleviating their rescuers of the financial stress of treatment so they can facilitate animal's adoption into a loving home.
See:
http://www.isfoundation.com/ISFEmergencyMedicalGrant

SPRINGSTEEN FOUNDATION

The Springsteen Foundation for the Humane Treatment of Animals, Inc. is organized exclusively for charitable purposes, making distributions to ARIZONA and MINNESOTA 501(c)(3) tax exempt organizations. The purpose shall be the promotion of public awareness and education of animal welfare and contribution to improvements in the welfare of both wildlife and domestic animals. Grant submission form can be found on the website and mailed to: The Springsteen Foundation for the Humane Treatment of Animals 1536 W Taro Lane Phoenix, AZ 85027
See: http://www.springsteenfoundation.org/index.php

THE STARK FAMILY FUND

The fund was established to assist community groups and charities in the Village of Bloomfield and Prince Edward County (ONTARIO, CANADA) in the areas of Animal Welfare as well as other community causes. Registered charities may send a letter of intent/form. Deadline of January 13th.
See: www.cfka.org

K.D. AND M.L. STEADLEY MEMORIAL TRUST

The Trust only supports charitable organizations operating in or near the city of Carthage, MISSOURI that work to promote the "well being of mankind and the general welfare of the community" including the prevention of cruelty to animals. Apply online. The deadlines are March 15 and November 15.
See:
https://www.bankofamerica.com/philanthropic/foundatio
n.go?fnId=148

STERKEL FUND

The Fund supports charitable purposes in Mansfield, Richland County OHIO. Funds animal welfare organizations among others. Deadlines and decision dates are in the 4th quarter. Applications must be submitted online.
See:
https://www.jpmorgan.com/pages/jpmorgan/private_ban
king/foundations/online_grant_application/search

FRANK H. STEWART TRUST

The Trust distributes grants for the purpose of purchasing land for public parks, recreation grounds, game refuges, fishing or propagation of fish, bird sanctuaries, or grounds for the protection and preservation of wildlife. Average grant size is $500,000. Applicants are generally 501(c)(3) organizations or any municipality therein and always based within NEW JERSEY - Gloucester County, Salem County Atlantic County, Cumberland County, and Cape May County. Applications submitted online are accepted year-round but there is an August 1 deadline.
See:
https://www.wellsfargo.com/privatefoundationgrants/ste
wart

C.H. STUART FOUNDATION
Supports charitable work in the township of Arcadia, NEW YORK and Wayne County, NEW YORK. Funds animal welfare organizations among others. Decision dates are in May and deadlines are in April. The Foundation is administered by J.P. Morgan, part of JPMorgan Chase & Co. Applications must be submitted online.
See:
https://www.jpmorgan.com/pages/jpmorgan/private_ban king/foundations/online_grant_application/search

STUDENT ANIMAL LEGAL DEFENSE FUND (SALDF)
Student Animal Legal Defense Fund ALDF promotes select scholarships, internships, jobs, and other professional development opportunities related to animal law. The Animal Legal Defense Fund (ALDF) encourages its chapters to plan programming on issues relating to ag gag legislation [animal abuse, food safety violations, and illegal working conditions, animal cruelty and agricultural practices that cause significant animal suffering, such as the use of crowded battery.] To assist student chapter efforts, ALDF offers project grants that fulfil the mission "to provide a forum for education, advocacy, and scholarship aimed at protecting the lives and advancing the interests of animals through the legal system, and raising the profile of the field of animal law."
See: http://aldf.org/resources/animal-law-events-opportunities/opportunities/

SUMMERLEE FOUNDATION

Grants have assisted a wide variety of programs, including companion animal issues, carnivore protection, sanctuary and refuge, and endangered species issues in North America and British Isles. The foundation wishes to alleviate fear, pain and suffering of animals and to promote animal protection and the prevention of cruelty to animals. Especially interested in spay/neuter programs, protection of feral cats, the suffering of captive animals such as dolphins and orcas, and the protection of mountain lions, coyotes and bobcats. Applicants must first contact the Animal Protection Program Director by phone 800-256-7515 or email mal3@summerlee.org. Cat grants average $5,000; other grants $10,000. Quarterly deadlines. See: http://www.summerlee.org/APP_GrantGuidelines.html

SUSIE'S FUND

Susie's Fund assists low-income cats and dogs in Hartford County, CONNECTICUT with spaying or neutering so as to alleviate unwanted litters of puppies and kittens. Grant application can be found online. See: http://www.queeniefoundation.org/susies-fund

DR. W.C. SWANSON FAMILY FOUNDATION, INC.

The Foundation supports anti-cruelty efforts, among other pursuits. At present, the Foundation is accepting grant applications by invitation only. There are no geographic restrictions or deadlines. See: http://www.swanfound.org/

THE F.W. SYMMES FOUNDATION
The F.W. Symmes Foundation funds organizations that work for the prevention of cruelty to children or animals. Funding limited to Greenville County, SOUTH CAROLINA. Applications accepted year round. Decisions made in spring and fall. Apply online.
See:
https://www.wellsfargo.com/privatefoundationgrants/symmes

ANN E. TALCOTT FUND
One of the Fund's focus areas is the prevention of cruelty to animals with a particular emphasis on indigent. Funding goes to 501(c)(3) organizations with past funding nationwide but emphasis on NEW JERSEY. July 22 deadline. Grants from $1,500 to $15,000. Online applications accepted year-round; awards made in September online.
See:
https://www.wellsfargo.com/privatefoundationgrants/talcott

DOREE TAYLOR CHARITABLE FOUNDATION
The mission of the Doree Taylor Charitable Foundation is to support charitable organizations including promoting the humane care of animals. The Foundation makes grants throughout MAINE, with a priority for the areas of Boothbay Harbor, Southport, and Brunswick. Apply online. The deadlines are June 1 and December 1. Operating support requests are encouraged.
See:
https://www.bankofamerica.com/philanthropic/foundation.go?fnId=83

FRED & HARRIET TAYLOR FOUNDATION
Supports charitable work in Hammondsport and Steuben Counties, NEW YORK. Funds animal welfare organizations among others. Decision dates are in July and deadlines are in June. Applications must be submitted online.
See: https://www.jpmorgan.com/pages/jpmorgan/private_banking/foundations/online_grant_application/search

TOSA FOUNDATION
The Foundation gives to animal welfare and wildlife causes, among other pursuits. Grants range in size from $100 to $30,000,000. Grants are given to pre-selected organizations with an emphasis on CALIFORNIA and MASSACHUSETTS.
Write: 3130 Alpine Rd Ste 288, PMB 705 Portola Valley, CA 94028

TRABANT NORTH KNOX COUNTY
The Trust supports charities in N. Knox County, INDIANA and vicinity; typically schools and municipalities. Funds animal welfare organizations among others. Decision dates are quarterly and there are no deadlines. The Foundation is administered by J.P. Morgan, part of JPMorgan Chase & Co. Applications must be submitted online.
See:
https://www.jpmorgan.com/pages/jpmorgan/private_banking/foundations/online_grant_application/search

THE TRIO ANIMAL FOUNDATION

The Trio Animal Foundation (TAF) is a 501(c)(3) charitable organization that assists shelters, rescues and individuals by paying the medical bills of homeless pets. Founded in honor of a very special dog named Trio, TAF also promotes adoption and responsible pet ownership, including spay and neuter. Trio Animal Foundation 516 North Ogden Ave. Suite 199 Chicago, IL 60642. See the online application at http://www.trioanimalfoundation.org/

EDWARD E. & HELEN TURNER BARTLETT

Supports charities focusing on the Creek County or the greater Tulsa, OKLAHOMA area. Funds animal welfare organizations among others. Decision dates vary and there are no deadlines. Contact: Edward & Helen Bartlett Foundation (formerly Edward E. Bartlett & Helen Turner Bartlett Foundation) P.O. Box 3627 Tulsa, OK United States 74101-3627 Telephone: (918) 744-0553

TWO MAUDS FOUNDATION

The Two Mauds, Inc. funds spay and neuter and other programs primarily in states east of the Mississippi. It was established by the late psychiatrist Dallas Pratt, founder of Argus Archives that sought to educate the public about the suffering of animals being used in experiments and relieve the exploitation and suffering of animals
Write: P.O. Box 792, Exmore, Virginia 23350-0792, Phone 757-442-9297 or email Jbmason40@verizon.net.

TWO SEVEN OH INC.

Grants awarded to MICHIGAN animal related organizations and programs. Applicants must be 501(c)(3) non-profits. Deadline is in September.
See: http://twosevenohinc.org/grants

UNIVERSAL PIG GENE INC.

Scholarships are awarded to college agriculture students studying swine management. For more information mail the International Boar Semen Scholarship Program at 30355 260th Street, Eldora, Iowa 50627.

USA EQUESTRIAN TRUST

The Trust makes grants from $3,000 to $20,000 in the U.S. to nonprofit organizations that work to enhance the sport of skilled horse-back riding. Deadline in May. Some funding is reserved for hunter/jumper activities in CALIFORNIA and NEVADA.
See: www.trusthorses.org

VACATION 4 A CAUSE

The organization partners with animal non-profits and other causes to raise money through travel. Every time a supporter books their vacation through Vacation 4 A Cause, the cause receives a significant donation. Donations are up to 8% of travel cost. Application form can be found on website. (An example of cause-marketing...See Notes at end.)
See: http://www.vacation4acause.com

THE VANCOUVER FOUNDATION ANIMAL WELFARE

The Animal Welfare grants program supports initiatives and programs in VANCOUVER, CANADA that benefit animals through research, outreach, education and direct care. Grant applications are due in September with final decisions being made in December.
See: http://www.vancouverfoundation.ca/grants/funding-guidelines

VOLUNTEER SERVICES TO ANIMALS

Volunteer Services for Animals (VSA) is a Rhode Island non-profit 501(c)(3) tax exempt humane organization established in 1979 to assist municipal animal shelters in providing adequate care and adoption outreach services for impounded animals. Funding goes to RHODE ISLAND based shelter organizations; providing adoption outreach services, companionship and medical assistance to animals waiting for new homes. Funding details can be accessed through the organization's website.
See:
http://www.volunteerservicesforanimals.org/index.html

THE TED & JANE VON VOIGTLANDER FOUNDATION

The Foundation supports animal advocacy, among other pursuits. Proposals are accepted by invitation only. Grants are awarded primarily in MICHIGAN with an emphasis on Livingston and Washtenaw Counties as well as the Petoskey/Bay Harbor area.
See: http://www.tjvv.org/

THE WAGMORE FOUNDATION

Provides funding for nonprofits who battle needless euthanasia of dogs and cats in Alachua County, FLORIDA. Special interest in community-based initiatives. Email info@wagmorefoundation.org to request a grant application.
See: http://www.wagmorefoundation.org/

THE S.K. WELLMAN FOUNDATION

The foundation funds animal welfare, among other causes, primarily in OHIO. Applicants must write for application form. Deadline is June 1. Grants are from $1,000 to $25,000. Write: Attention: Ethel Pearson, PO Box 32554, Euclid, Ohio 44132-0554.

WELLS COLLEGE TRUST
Supports charitable purposes. Funds animal welfare organizations among others. NEW YORK state only. Decision dates are in November and deadlines are in October. The Foundation is administered by J.P. Morgan, part of JPMorgan Chase & Co. Applications must be submitted online.
See: https://www.jpmorgan.com/pages/jpmorgan/private_banking/foundations/online_grant_application/search

THE TOBY WELLS FOUNDATION
The Toby Wells Foundation welcomes funding requests from recognized 501 (c) (3) non-profit organizations operating programs within San Diego County for initiatives that support work that enhances the lives of animals, among other pursuits. Grants made no more than $2,500. Deadline September 5th.
See: http://tobywells.org/home

WEST MARINE
West Marine makes Marine Conservation grants to support conservation and recreational fishing projects that promote health marine habitats and stocks across the U.S. Grants are for up to $5,000.
See: http://www.westmarine.com/BlueFuture/Grants-Sponsorships

WIEDERHOLD FOUNDATION VIA COMMUNITY FOUNDATION OF NORTHWEST CONNECTICUT

The John T. and Jane A. Wiederhold Foundation was created for the purpose of protecting and improving the welfare of animals of all kinds with a focus on cats and dogs, the promotion of veterinary programs and, the protection of wildlife, including endangered species, flora and fauna. Grant applications to the Foundation are by invitation only. Most awards are to Connecticut, New England or national organizations.
See: https://cfnwct.org/wiederhold-foundation

WILDLIFE REHABILITATION IN THE DISTRICT OF COLUMBIA

The District Department of the Environment (DDOE) makes grants available to nonprofit organizations to provide for wildlife rehabilitation services in the DISTRICT OF COLUMBIA for sick, injured, and orphaned native and naturalized wild animals. The applicant must have a wildlife rehabilitator license; existing facilities, located in DC, triage and treat sick, injured, and orphaned wildlife; and a support staff trained in and experienced with wildlife rehabilitation. For additional information regarding this RFA, please contact DDOE.
See: www.ddoe.dc.gov

WILLISTON STAR FUND

The Fund's Community Enhancement Grant is intended to take mini steps to make Williston, NORTH DAKOTA a better place by helping new and existing businesses to succeed, make their properties more attractive to their customers, and to make the community more attractive to potential new businesses, employees, residents and visitors. The STAR Fund will match the investment of any non-profit group in commercial and industrial zoned property projects on a 1:2 basis with a maximum of $10,000 per project. Applicant's minimum out of pocket project expense shall total $20,000, with a mini-match cap of $200,000 per calendar year available. Deadline of December 15th. See website for application details.
See: www.willistonwire.com/Programs/Williston-STAR-Fund

EARL M. WILSON TRUST

The Trust funds organizations that prevent cruelty to animals within Buncombe County, NORTH CAROLINA. Eight grants are awarded each year with an average amount of $5,000. Applicants must be a 501(c)(3) organizations located within the specified area. Submissions are accepted year-round though they must be received by June 15th in order to be reviewed in July. Apply online.
See:
https://www.wellsfargo.com/privatefoundationgrants/wilson

THE WINN FELINE FOUNDATION AND MILLER TRUST

Winn Feline Foundation has provided and continues to provide significant information veterinarians need to care for cats. Winn-supported health studies have helped veterinarians improve the diagnosis and treatment of many diseases and conditions. The Foundation has awarded grants for scientific studies, encouraging veterinarians and researchers to focus attention on the health needs of cats. There are three types of grants with varying deadlines and review schedules.

See: http://www.winnfelinefoundation.org/grants/grant-process

WINNER'S CIRCLE SCHOLARSHIP PROGRAM

Scholarships are awarded to U.S. fourth year veterinary medicine students who are accredited by American Veterinarian Medical Association (AVMA). For more information write Winner's Circle Scholarship Program, 1818 Versailles Road, Lexington, Kentucky 40504.

WISCONSIN STATE RABBIT BREEDERS ASSOCIATION

The Association's grant program's main objective is to promote and perpetuate the rabbit hobby or industry in WISCONSIN. The Entrepreneurial Grant is designed to provide a youth member (14 to 20 years of age) of the WSRBA with funding to develop and work through a project that will benefit the WSRBA, it's members and/or the rabbit industry in WI. Applicants will be judged on the impact the proposed project has on others. Grants range in amount from $100 to $500. Deadline of July 1st. See website for application details.

See:
www.wsrba.org/images/WSRBAentrepreneurgrantNew2009.pdf

HERBERT A. AND ADRIAN W. WOODS FOUNDATION

The Herbert A. and Adrian W. Woods Foundation supports charitable organizations primarily in the greater St. Louis, MISSOURI area including animal welfare causes. September 1 deadline. Apply online, request funding for special projects, matching or operating funds.
See:
https://www.bankofamerica.com/philanthropic/foundatio n.go?fnId=7

GEORGE & FAY YOUNG FOUNDATION, INC.

The Foundation makes grants for programs in which animal welfare is the core component,as well as programs that promote the importance of the relationship between humans and animals. Most funding goes to TEXAS but also elsewhere. Deadline in September.
See: www.gfyfoundation.org

1-800-PetMeds®

The company's "Change a Pet's Life" contest was created to sponsor the medical treatments and adoption fees of several adoptable pets within the UNITED STATES. Animal shelters and rescue groups may apply to have their animals added to the list of submissions in January, with voting ending on January 22nd. The three pets with the most votes win grants for their medical treatment or adoption fees. See website for application details.
See: www.petmeds.org

786 FOUNDATION

786 Foundation was established to provide funding for the charitable purposes including animal welfare for education, general operating support, matching/challenge support and scholarship funds. Giving is across the UNITED STATES. An application form not required. Interested applicants should submit one copy of a proposal. There is no deadline. Call 608.232.2009 for more information.

786 Foundation
Attn.: Jennifer Ridley-Hanson
c/o BMO Private Bank
P.O. Box 8988
Madison, WI 53708-8988

400 PAWS, INC.

400 Paws, Inc. helps to fund 501c3 nonprofit animal shelters and rescues that are not funded by government and are in FLORIDA: Escambia, Santa Rosa, Walton and Okaloosa Counties that provide for animals (dogs & cats, equine or wildlife). The mission is to use publicity and outreach to raise funds for qualified non-profit animal organizations on a yearly basis by vote of active members, while educating the community regarding the importance of animal welfare and the need for financial assistance within the animal shelters and rescue groups. Application process begins with a letter of inquiry and submission of the 501c3 document. See: www.400paws.org.

OTHER RESOURCES:

GOVERNMENT AND COMMUNITY GRANTS

A rural municipality might look into federal USDA Community Facility grants for renovations or construction. Some states, like Georgia, Missouri and Michigan, and some Canadian provincial governments, offer grants to licensed animal shelters and nonprofit animal rescue groups for pet sterilization programs. Go to your state or province's webpage and look for animal grants - possibly under the Department of Agriculture or Department of Health. In addition, over twenty states, including Ohio, Arizona, Texas, Kentucky, etc. offer special pet license plates as a way to raise and then distribute grants to spay and neuter programs or other animal welfare activities; the application process differs state to state.

You may also contact your area's community foundation and see if your project is eligible. A community foundation may pay for a new computer or renovation but may not pay for operational costs. Some community foundations like the Rhode Island Foundation (See http://www.rifoundation.org/WorkingTogether/ForNonprofits/GrantOpportunities/ProgramforAnimalWelfare.aspx) manages funds from various donors dedicated to animal welfare.

CLOSED GRANTS

Some Foundations may only give to preselected organizations or publicize that no applications will be accepted. In this case, if they are in your service area, you may wish to keep an eye on their activities and note whether the trustees, areas of interest and application process changes over time. And in some cases it may be appropriate to add the trustees or foundation to your organization's newsletter mailing list. Some foundations' assets change over time. Some foundations change as the next generation assumes leadership. You may want to check their website or 990 each year to see if they have resumed giving to applicants.

FUNDRAISING

Many foundations like to see that your nonprofit has already raised some funds toward your project. If a grant maker asks for a budget and expects a local match – that is the money you raised from other sources. Example: If you are proposing a $10,000 project, for example, and the funder requires a 10% local match, you will need to show that you have already raised $1,000 through fundraising for this the project and are requesting a grant of $9,000.

Nonprofits raise funds in multiple ways - events, annual gifts, memorials, online giving, etc. Do you ask donors for the name and address of the person(s) to be notified if a donor makes a gift in honor or in memory of someone? Do you send out a year end annual appeal letter by mail or email to past supporters (past donors, volunteers, current and past staff, current and past board members, vendors, past and current interns, etc.)?

Busy people and those that act on impulse enjoy e-giving – it is quick and easy. Do you have a Paypal™ Donate Now button on your webpage? Or are you able to receive donations via smart phones and receive PCI compliant donations (meeting Payment Card Industry Data Security Standards to ensure security)? People can make gifts easily using Network for Good (www.networkforgood.com) among others. The donation minus a transaction fee is deposited directly into your nonprofit's bank account. Be sure to read all the instructions and agreement language. You also may wish to look into accepting donations via QR codes or Electronic Funds Transfer (EFT). You can even set up monthly gifts instead of onetime gifts.

Other sources of funding for nonprofits raising money for rescues or shelter operations may include social media fundraising or crowdfunding. Just some of the sites to explore are: www.razoo.com/p/for_nonprofits, www.giveforward.com, www.fundrazr.com, www.fundraisingforacause.com, www.crowdrise.com, www.LoveAnimals.com, www.indiegogo.com, www.zip.kiva.org, www.justgive.org, etc. Be sure to check and compare transaction fees.

You can also promote a fundraising event using a site like EventBrite. (Note there is even a way for people who cannot attend the event to make a donation without buying a ticket. (See: www.eventbrite.com/l/npo/.)

Consider cause marketing with area businesses (local businesses or corporations agree to give some $ for each item sold to your cause; the business gets good publicity, your group gets some money.)

A pay it forward program allows people to pay their bill and then pay the fee for the next customer (such as for spaying/neutering). Another example, if a feed store sells dog food, a customer can be encouraged to buy their bag and pay for a 2nd bag which is given to the shelter.

Register your nonprofit at org.amazon.com (See: http://smile.amazon.com/about) to secure donations from Amazon shoppers via the AmazonSmile™ Foundation for your organization. Then spread the word electronically among your supporters that if they shop Amazon to log in to shop using smile.amazon.com and then select your charity. Think of all the holiday shoppers that make purchases through Amazon each winter!

Nonprofits can also update their profile on GuideStar.org. Potential donors may search GuideStar looking for organization's whose causes fit their values. Donors may make a gift through GuideStar (See: http://www.guidestar.org/rxg/help/faqs/on-line-donations/index.aspx#faq1812.) Create an account and claim your nonprofit, then click on update Nonprofit Report to set up your organization's profile. Fill out the GuideStar Exchange Form (GX) to provide additional information about your organization including uploading documents.

STAY IN TOUCH

To be added to a mailing list about future nonprofit management or fundraising tools, please share your information by emailing <u>info@grant-write.com</u> or writing Pamela Burke, P.O. Box 291, Remus, Michigan 49340.

Also feel free to share a summary of your successful funding strategies.

ABOUT THE AUTHOR

The author, Pamela Burke, has worked with, and for, nonprofit and charitable organizations her entire life. She began searching for funding and writing grants in 1978 – first as a volunteer, later as an employee, and for the last two decades as a self-employed grant writer and fund development consultant. As a technical assistance provider her mission is to improve the quality of life in communities by building the organizational capacity of nonprofits – especially those serving rural areas. When not working, you can find her planning her next trip, working in the garden, dabbling in the arts, kayaking and volunteering.

Disclaimer
This publication only includes a sampling of resources available; there are other resources for groups and individuals not included in this publication. For the resources included in this publication, the information contained is not meant to be taken as an endorsement, recommendation or as verification that funding is available to you or your group or those you wish to help. Funding programs change over time and amounts fluctuate with revenue changes; assistance programs are often dependent on earnings from fundraising events, donations, investment income or other. The programs also have various eligibility requirements. The information is shared only as potential options to be further explored. Most of the organizations listed here welcome gifts and donations; please consider giving as well as receiving.

31598187R10082

Made in the USA
Middletown, DE
06 May 2016